The Weight of Capital

The Weight of Capital

Stewardship, Responsibility, and the Systems We Shape

Heather Desjardins

Shepherds of Capital Publishing

Published by Shepherds of Capital Publishing
A division of Shepherds of Capital Holdings LLC
Clearwater, Florida, United States

First Edition
ISBN (Paperback): 979-8-9957723-0-9
ISBN (Hardcover): 979-8-9957723-4-7
ISBN (eBook): 979-8-9957723-2-3

Printed in the United States of America

For bulk orders, special editions, or institutional inquiries, contact:
publishing@ShepherdsofCapital.com

Library of Congress Control Number: 2026910145

Capital allocation is the most powerful force shaping the future that no one sees.

Contents

Introduction

The Weight No One Talks About

Capital is typically discussed in terms of performance, allocation, and return. It is measured, optimized, and compared across markets and institutions. What is less often examined is its consequence. Every allocation sets direction. Every decision reinforces a structure. Over time, those decisions accumulate, shaping systems, institutions, and outcomes far beyond the moment in which they are made.

Each day, vast quantities of capital move through the global financial system. Trillions of dollars shift between markets, industries, and asset classes as investors evaluate risk and pursue opportunity. These movements are so continuous that they appear routine, part of the background function of modern economic life. Financial commentary reflects this orientation. Capital is described as responding to incentives embedded in prices, interest rates, and market signals. Charts fluctuate, models adjust, and strategies evolve in response to changing conditions.

There is truth in this view. Markets do exhibit patterns, and disciplined analysis is essential for navigating uncertainty. Yet describing capital only through this lens obscures something more fundamental. Capital does not simply respond to systems. It participates in shaping them.

When capital flows into a sector at scale, conditions within that sector begin to change. Pricing adjusts, access shifts, and incentives realign. In residential housing, for example, sustained institutional investments can alter ownership patterns and affordability within local markets. These outcomes are not incidental. They reflect the cumulative effect of allocation decisions operating within a defined structure.

This dynamic extends across the broader economy. Capital directed toward certain industries accelerates their development, attracts talent, and builds supporting infrastructure. Capital withheld from other areas limits expansion and, over time, narrows the range of viable outcomes. What appears as a discrete activity, evaluated transaction by transaction, accumulates into patterns that shape the structure of economic life.

Within financial institutions, these decisions often appear technical and procedural. Analysts assess data, portfolio managers weigh competing opportunities, and investment committees review projections designed to estimate risk and return. These processes are necessary. They enable capital to be deployed with discipline in complex, uncertain environments. Yet when viewed collectively, their influence is far greater than their individual components suggest.

The cumulative movement of capital determines which ideas receive support, which institutions gain durability, and which forms of economic activity are allowed to expand. Infrastructure is built because capital finances it. Innovation advances when investment sustains it. Entire industries emerge through repeated allocation, while others recede when that support is absent.

The absence of capital also carries consequences. Communities without sustained investment often struggle to maintain economic vitality. Viable ideas can disappear when financing fails to materialize. Institutions capable of contributing to long-term stability may weaken simply because resources are not directed toward them in time.

These outcomes rarely result from a single decision. They emerge gradually as thousands of allocations accumulate across time. Each may appear modest within the context of global markets. Together, they shape the trajectory of systems.

What remains less examined is the responsibility embedded within this process. Capital is typically treated as a mechanism to be optimized, rather than a force whose direction carries structural consequence. The distinction is not semantic. It defines the difference between viewing capital as a tool and recognizing it as an influence.

This book examines how capital moves, how patterns of allocation form, and how those patterns shape the systems in which economic life unfolds. It does not seek to redefine finance, but to clarify the role it already plays.

Capital directs outcomes over time.

The question is whether that direction is fully understood.

Part I

The Nature of Capital

"Consumption is the sole end and purpose of all production."

Adam Smith

The Wealth of Nations

Chapter 1

Capital Is Not Neutral

Capital exists to be directed. It does not remain idle or operate in isolation. It is accumulated, allocated, and redeployed through systems that determine how resources move across economies. These movements are not neutral. They reflect decisions about what will be built, sustained, or allowed to diminish over time.

Capital is often described as money, assets, or financial resources available for investment. While these definitions are functionally correct, they are incomplete. Capital is not defined solely by its form, but by its capacity to direct human effort. It determines where labor is applied, which ideas receive support, and how resources are organized. In this sense, capital is not simply a store of value. It is a coordinating force that shapes activity over time.

Modern finance often treats capital as a neutral force moving through markets according to predictable rules. In financial commentary, capital is frequently described in mechanical language. Investors pursue returns, companies raise funding, and asset prices rise or fall as markets respond to new information, changes in interest rates, and shifting economic expectations. Analysts construct models to capture these movements, while economists describe cycles and trends as if capital behaves according to patterns that can be observed and measured.

This framework serves an important purpose. Financial systems are complex, and disciplined analysis allows participants to navigate uncertainty. Investors rely on models and historical data to estimate risk and evaluate opportunities. Institutions establish structured processes for allocating resources responsibly across portfolios that must perform under constantly changing market conditions. Without these tools, modern financial markets could not operate at their current scale and speed.

Yet this framework is incomplete. It treats capital as if it operates independently of consequence, rather than as a force that shapes systems over time. Each allocation does more than respond to conditions. It shapes them. The movement of capital influences which institutions gain durability, which ideas receive support, and which forms of economic activity expand or recede. These effects are not always visible in the moment, but they accumulate and shape outcomes.

At the same time, the language used to describe capital can sometimes obscure a deeper reality. Capital is said to move toward opportunity and away from risk, guided by the incentives embedded within prices and expected returns. The metaphor often used is that of water traveling through pipes, seeking the most efficient path through a system of channels and valves.

But capital does not move on its own.

Every allocation represents a decision, and behind each decision lies a set of assumptions about value, opportunity, risk, and the future. Those assumptions decide which ideas receive support and which remain unrealized. They influence which businesses expand, which industries develop, and which technologies receive the resources required to move from experimentation into everyday life.

Systems do not emerge all at once. They are formed through the repeated allocation of capital over time. Each decision reinforces structures, directs resources to particular uses, and establishes patterns that become embedded in markets and institutions. As these patterns accumulate, they shape the conditions under which future decisions are made, creating feedback loops that strengthen some outcomes while limiting others. In this sense, capital does far more than move through markets. It takes part in building them.

The effects of capital allocation rarely appear immediately. Individual decisions often seem modest when viewed in isolation. A venture investment supports a new company. A bank extends credit to a growing enterprise. A pension fund adjusts its portfolio, increasing exposure to one sector while reducing exposure to another. Within the daily operations of financial institutions, these decisions appear routine, part of the ordinary rhythm of financial management.

Over time, however, the accumulation of these decisions produces powerful results. Industries expand because capital consistently supports their development. Others gradually disappear when financing becomes scarce. Regions prosper when investment sustains infrastructure, research, and enterprise. Communities struggle when the capital required for renewal and growth fails to arrive.

When viewed across decades, the pattern of capital allocation begins to resemble a map of economic possibility.

Technological revolutions rarely emerge in isolation. They develop when capital supports experimentation, development, and the scaling of new ideas. Industrial transformation occurs when investors finance infrastructure, production networks, and distribution systems that support new forms of economic activity. Even cultural and scientific institutions often depend on capital deployed with patience and long-term vision.

History provides many examples of this constructive power. Financial resources helped finance the railroads that connected continents and expanded global trade. Capital supported the development of electrical infrastructure that transformed cities and industries. Investment in scientific research made advances in medicine that extended life expectancy across much of the world.

Yet capital has also contributed to very different outcomes when guided by different incentives.

Financial history contains numerous periods in which capital flowed aggressively toward speculative opportunities that ultimately proved fragile. Episodes of rapid expansion fueled by leverage and optimism have sometimes created systems that appeared stable for years before revealing underlying weaknesses. When confidence shifted, those systems unraveled, spreading instability across markets and societies.

In each of these moments, the mechanism was the same. Capital moved toward certain opportunities and away from others. What differed was the philosophy guiding those decisions.

When capital is directed with patience and a long-term perspective, it can support institutions that endure across generations. Universities, transportation networks, research laboratories, and public health systems often emerge from capital invested with the understanding that the most meaningful outcomes may unfold over years or decades. These institutions rarely arise from short-term thinking. They are built through decisions made with an awareness that capital can establish foundations upon which future progress depends.

At other times, capital is guided by incentives that emphasize speed, momentum, and immediate advantage. Under those conditions, markets can become increasingly fragile. Risk accumulates gradually, leverage expands, and participants begin responding to similar signals while pursuing similar strategies. Systems that appear stable for extended periods can eventually reveal vulnerabilities that were difficult to recognize while they were forming.

The distinction between these outcomes is rarely obvious at the moment decisions are made. Financial allocations often appear similar on the surface. They involve projections, expected returns, and analytical models designed to estimate uncertain futures. Yet over time, the cumulative consequences of those decisions reveal something important.

Recognizing this reality invites a broader perspective on the role of capital within modern societies. Discussions of finance often focus on performance metrics, market efficiency, and the pursuit of returns. These considerations are essential to the functioning of markets, yet they capture only part of the influence embedded within capital allocation.

Behind every investment lies a judgment about the future. Investors form expectations about which technologies will matter, which industries will grow, and which institutions will remain durable. Information, incentives, and the prevailing ideas of a particular era shape these judgments. Repeated across thousands of decisions and across decades, those judgments influence the trajectory of entire economic systems.

The scale of this influence has grown dramatically in the modern era. Pension funds, sovereign wealth funds, insurance institutions, and global asset managers now oversee pools of capital measured in trillions of dollars. Their allocation decisions influence the cost of capital for companies, the development of infrastructure, and the availability of financing across regions of the world. Through these decisions, capital shapes not only markets but also the opportunities available to future generations.

Yet the deeper implications of this influence are rarely discussed directly within the language of finance. Capital is often described primarily as a resource that can be measured, priced, and optimized through analytical models. Beneath those models lies something more fundamental: the accumulated effort of individuals and societies whose labor, savings, and enterprise created the wealth that financial systems now allocate.

Retirement savings represent decades of work by millions of individuals. University endowments reflect generations of philanthropy and intellectual investment. Sovereign funds represent national resources held in trust for future citizens. These pools of capital carry the expectations of those who created them and the hopes of those who depend upon them.

When capital is directed thoughtfully, it can strengthen institutions capable of serving communities for generations. When it is directed carelessly, the same force can produce fragile structures built on speculation or incentives that reward short-term gain at the expense of long-term stability. The difference between these outcomes rarely appears immediately. It emerges gradually as the effects of capital allocation compound across time.

For this reason, the true weight of capital cannot be measured solely in dollars. Its weight lies in the consequences created by where it is placed. Each allocation contributes to patterns that shape the economic and institutional landscape inherited by the future.

Understanding this weight is the first step toward stewardship.

Stewardship begins with the recognition that capital is never neutral. It carries the accumulated effort of those who created it and the expectations of those who depend upon it. The savings of workers, the endowments of institutions, and the reserves of nations all represent human effort stored for future use. Those entrusted with directing capital, therefore, participate in decisions that influence far more than financial performance.

Their choices help determine which institutions endure, which industries develop, and which opportunities become available to the generations that follow.

Recognizing this responsibility changes the way capital must be understood. It is no longer merely a resource to be deployed efficiently. It becomes a force capable of shaping the architecture of societies themselves.

This realization raises a deeper question.

If capital holds such influence over the structure of the modern world, how did it acquire that reach in the first place?

Modern financial systems did not emerge suddenly. They evolved gradually over centuries of experimentation, expanding societies' ability to mobilize resources across distance, risk, and time. The institutions that now move trillions of dollars across global markets each day began with far simpler tools developed by merchants seeking practical solutions to trade challenges.

Understanding the weight capital carries today, therefore, requires stepping back to examine the origins of the systems that allow capital to move on such a scale.

The story begins with the earliest attempts to extend economic activity beyond the limits of place.

It begins with the creation of financial systems themselves.

Chapter 2

The First Expansion of Capital

For most of human history, capital was local.

Wealth certainly existed, and societies had long recognized forms of value that could be stored, exchanged, and accumulated. Land produced agricultural output. Livestock represented mobile wealth that could be traded or transferred. Precious metals served as durable stores of value and mediums of exchange. In early civilizations, these assets allowed communities to organize economic life and sustain trade within relatively small geographic regions.

Yet wealth in these early systems remained closely tied to place. A farmer's prosperity was measured in fields and harvests. A merchant might accumulate goods within a warehouse or maintain modest reserves of gold or silver. A ruler's resources depended largely on the taxes that could be collected from the territory under their control. Economic activity, therefore, operated within boundaries defined by geography, security, and the speed at which information could travel.

Trade between regions did exist, sometimes across remarkable distances. Caravan routes linked parts of Asia and Europe, via the Middle East, across overland networks that would later be known collectively as the Silk Road. Maritime trade connected Mediterranean ports and gradually extended toward India and Southeast Asia. These networks enabled the exchange of spices, textiles, metals, and luxury goods across continents.

Yet the logistical realities of moving goods and money across long distances imposed significant limits on the scale of economic activity.

Transporting valuable commodities was difficult and dangerous. Goods moved by ship, by package, or by wagon along routes that were often poorly maintained and exposed to theft or conflict. Communication between cities could take weeks or even months. The movement of large quantities of gold or silver along trade routes exposed merchants to piracy, banditry, and loss.

In such an environment, capital remained tethered to geography.

If a merchant wished to finance a trading venture, the funds had to be assembled locally. If a ruler required resources to support military campaigns or public works, the necessary wealth had to be raised through taxation or borrowed from lenders who physically possessed the required assets nearby. The scale of enterprise was therefore constrained by the resources that could be gathered within a relatively limited radius.

For centuries, this limitation defined the outer boundary of economic possibility. Economic growth could occur, but it expanded slowly because the mechanisms for mobilizing capital over long distances had not developed.

Then, gradually and almost quietly, something began to change.

Beginning in the late medieval period and accelerating during the Renaissance, a series of financial innovations began reshaping the flow of capital through society. These developments did not initially appear revolutionary. They emerged as practical solutions to the problems faced by merchants operating in expanding trade networks. Yet over time, those solutions would transform the nature of capital itself.

One of the most important early developments occurred in the merchant city of Florence.

During the fifteenth century, Florence stood at the center of one of Europe's most dynamic commercial economies. Florentine merchants traded textiles, metals, spices, and luxury goods across the Mediterranean and throughout Europe's major trading centers. Commercial networks connected Florence with cities such as Venice, Rome, Geneva, Bruges, and London, forming an expanding web of exchange linking distant markets.

As trade expanded, merchants encountered a persistent problem. Moving money across long distances was difficult and dangerous.

Transporting gold or silver physically between cities exposed merchants to enormous risks. Ships carrying precious metals could be lost at sea. Caravans could be attacked along remote routes. Even when shipments arrived safely, the process remained slow and costly. Commerce needed a safer, more efficient way to transfer value.

The solution emerged as a financial instrument, the bill of exchange, that quietly reshaped the architecture of trade. Through this mechanism, a merchant could deposit funds with a banking house in one city and receive a written document representing that value. That document could then be presented at a related banking office in another city, where the equivalent amount could be withdrawn in local currency. Instead of transporting precious metals across dangerous routes, merchants could transfer value through trusted financial networks.

To modern readers, this innovation may appear modest. In reality, it represented a profound transformation.

For the first time, value could move through systems of trust and information rather than through the physical movement of precious metals. Capital began traveling through relationships between institutions rather than through wagons and ships.

Commerce expanded almost immediately.

Merchants gained the ability to conduct transactions across multiple cities more quickly and securely. Banking houses became intermediaries connecting distant markets and enabling trade networks to function more efficiently. The financial infrastructure supporting commerce began extending beyond local boundaries.

Capital was beginning to detach itself from geography.

Among the Florentine banking families that participated in this transformation, none became more influential than the Medici family.

Founded in the late fourteenth century, the Medici bank developed one of the most sophisticated financial networks of its era. By the mid-fifteenth century, the institution operated branches across Europe's major commercial centers. These branches functioned as nodes within a coordinated financial system. Funds deposited in one city could be transferred to another through the bank's internal accounting structure.

Merchants conducting international trade could finance shipments, settle accounts, and manage currency exchanges through the Medici network.

In effect, the Medici bank created one of the earliest multinational financial institutions.

Its influence extended far beyond commercial transactions. European rulers relied on banking houses to finance wars, infrastructure, and administrative operations. Through these relationships, financial institutions became deeply intertwined with political authority and social power.

The Medici family's reach expanded accordingly.

Their wealth enabled them to become patrons of art, architecture, and scholarship. The Renaissance itself was shaped in part by the financial resources flowing through networks such as the Medici bank. Artists, including Michelangelo and Leonardo da Vinci, produced works under patronage systems made possible by capital controlled by influential families.

Banking was not merely financing trade.

It was shaping culture.

The Medici story illustrates a deeper transformation occurring within the economy. As banking networks expanded, financial power was increasingly concentrated within institutions capable of directing capital flows across regions. Decisions made within banking offices in Florence could influence markets and merchants hundreds of miles away.

The scale of capital was beginning to grow, and with that expansion came a corresponding increase in the influence carried by those who directed its movement.

Over the centuries that followed, financial systems continued to evolve. New institutions and innovations expanded both the reach and complexity of capital. Among the most important developments was the emergence of joint-stock companies during the seventeenth century.

As global trade expanded, commercial ventures began requiring levels of capital far beyond what individual merchants or banking families could provide. Maritime expeditions, overseas trading posts, and international trade networks demanded enormous financial resources. No single investor could easily bear the risks or supply the required capital alone.

The solution emerged through a structure that allowed large groups of investors to pool resources within a single enterprise.

Joint-stock companies divided ownership into shares, each representing a proportional claim to profits. Investors could purchase these shares, providing capital to the enterprise while sharing in the financial returns generated by its activities.

One of the most famous early examples was the Dutch East India Company, based in Amsterdam and established in 1602.

The company received a charter granting it authority to conduct trade throughout large regions of Asia and establish trading posts across multiple territories. Financing these activities required substantial capital, which the company raised by issuing shares to investors. Those shares could then be bought and sold among investors, creating one of the earliest functioning public markets for financial assets.

The implications were enormous.

For the first time, capital could be assembled from large groups of investors and deployed toward ventures operating across oceans and continents. Trade expanded dramatically as European companies established global networks for the exchange of goods.

Stock exchanges soon emerged in cities such as Amsterdam and London, providing centralized venues where investors could trade shares in companies and other financial instruments. These markets introduced liquidity into the financial system, allowing capital to move more freely between opportunities while enabling investors to diversify their risk.

Financial markets were beginning to take recognizable shape.

By the time the Industrial Revolution emerged during the eighteenth and nineteenth centuries, these financial structures had matured into systems capable of mobilizing capital on a scale that earlier societies could scarcely imagine.

Railroads stretched across nations. Factories transformed production. Steam engines reshaped transportation and industry. Urban centers expanded as manufacturing economies replaced agricultural ones. All of these developments required enormous quantities of capital.

Banks financed infrastructure projects. Investors purchased shares in industrial enterprises. Governments issued bonds to fund public works and national development. Financial systems mobilized resources across entire societies, enabling economic transformation on an unprecedented scale.

Economic growth accelerated as capital moved into industries that would reshape the modern world.

Yet beneath these dramatic changes, the underlying dynamic remained consistent with the pattern first emerging in Renaissance banking networks. As the scale of capital expanded, so did the influence carried by those who directed it.

Those responsible for allocating capital were not merely participating in economic activity. They were helping determine which technologies would be developed, which industries would flourish, and which regions would experience economic transformation.

Capital had evolved from a local resource into a force capable of shaping entire economies.

Today, the scale of that influence has grown far beyond the world imagined by Renaissance bankers or early industrial financiers. Global financial markets move trillions of dollars each day. Investment funds deploy capital across continents in search of opportunity. Corporations operate within supply chains that span dozens of countries. Financial transactions occur in fractions of a second through digital systems connecting institutions across the world.

The financial architecture that began forming in merchant cities centuries ago has expanded into a vast global network.

Yet despite the technological sophistication of modern markets, the underlying principle remains unchanged.

Capital moves through systems designed and governed by people. And the direction of those flows carries consequences far beyond individual investments.

The early expansion of banking reminds us that the power of capital did not emerge suddenly in the modern era. It developed gradually through innovations that expanded society's ability to mobilize resources, finance enterprises, and support economic growth. Each stage of this evolution increased the scale at which capital could operate.

With each expansion in scale, the responsibility carried by those directing capital grew heavier.

Capital now moves faster, farther, and in greater quantities than at any point in human history. Its influence touches nearly every dimension of economic life.

To understand the weight capital carries today, one must first understand how it was created. The systems that now direct trillions of dollars across global markets began with a simple transformation, the moment when value first learned to move beyond the limits of place.

Once that transformation began, the scale of capital continued expanding for centuries. Understanding where that expansion ultimately led is the next step in understanding the world of modern finance.

Chapter 3

The Power of Allocation

When most people think about capital, they think about money. They picture balance sheets, market charts, investment accounts, or the large financial institutions that dominate the modern economic landscape. In this view, capital appears primarily as a quantity, something accumulated, measured, invested, and tracked through numbers on a screen. Wealth becomes an amount. Performance becomes a return. Success becomes growth.

This understanding is not entirely wrong. Capital can be counted, priced, and measured across portfolios, institutions, and markets. Financial systems depend upon this ability to quantify resources and compare outcomes. Without such measurement, modern finance could not function with discipline or coherence.

Yet capital is not defined primarily by its quantity. Its deeper significance lies in what it allows societies to do.

Capital becomes powerful only when it is directed.

Someone must decide where it goes, and those decisions determine what becomes possible. At that moment, capital ceases to be abstract. Every financial system, regardless of its complexity, ultimately rests on a simple human act: allocation.

Capital does not move on its own. It moves because individuals and institutions determine which opportunities deserve resources and which do not. These decisions often occur quietly within organizations whose work rarely attracts public attention, yet they shape the trajectory of economies and the structure of entire industries.

Ideas alone do not transform the world.

Every innovation, enterprise, and infrastructure project requires resources long before it produces visible results. An engineer may develop a promising technology. An entrepreneur may identify a new market. A community may envision the construction of roads, ports, hospitals, schools, or public utilities. Each of these possibilities requires capital to move from idea into reality.

Allocation, therefore, serves as the bridge between imagination and reality. It determines which ideas become institutions and which remain unrealized. It determines whether a possibility is merely discussed or built, tested, expanded, and sustained over time. In that sense, allocation is not simply a financial function. It is one of the primary ways a society expresses its priorities.

In modern financial systems, the allocation process often appears procedural. Investment managers analyze financial statements. Economists produce forecasts. Committees debate risks and expected returns. The language used in these discussions can seem technical and distant from everyday life. Allocations are framed as percentages, risk exposures, and performance expectations.

Yet beneath this analytical structure lies something far more consequential.

Each decision about where capital should flow determines which possibilities move forward and which remain unexplored. The process may appear technical, but its effects are structural. Capital does not simply reward what already exists. It determines what will be given the chance to endure.

For every enterprise that grows into a lasting institution,

countless other ideas never receive the resources required to develop. For every technological breakthrough that transforms industries, many innovations fail to attract sufficient investment to leave the laboratory. For every region that becomes a center of commerce and opportunity, another region struggles to attract capital at all.

These outcomes are not merely the product of chance. They reflect the cumulative effect of allocation.

Over time, patterns of allocation begin to shape entire economic landscapes. When capital flows consistently toward particular sectors, those sectors expand. Talent gathers where investment is available. Supply chains develop around growing industries. Supporting technologies emerge to serve those markets. Universities, training programs, and local institutions begin orienting themselves around the opportunities capital has reinforced.

What begins as a cluster of investments gradually becomes an ecosystem.

This is one of the clearest ways to understand the power of allocation. Capital does not simply fund individual transactions. It creates momentum. It attracts additional resources. It signals to other participants where opportunity is believed to exist. Over time, repeated allocations begin to build structures far larger than any single decision.

The development of modern technology industries offers a vivid illustration of this process. Decades of sustained investment in computing, communications, semiconductors, software, and digital infrastructure have gradually produced sectors that now define the global economy. Early investors could not have predicted the full scale of the transformation that would follow. Many companies funded during the early years of technological development failed.

Yet the continued flow of capital toward innovation allowed experimentation to persist long enough for extraordinary successes to emerge.

Those successes reshaped communication, commerce, transportation, media, and information itself. What began as uncertain experiments evolved into the technological foundation of modern society. This transformation did not occur simply because innovative ideas existed. It occurred because capital was repeatedly allocated toward their development, allowing time, talent, and infrastructure to gather around them.

In this way, allocation determines more than financial performance.

It determines which futures are given the chance to arrive.

The influence of allocation becomes even clearer when financial systems misallocate capital. History contains many examples of periods in which enthusiasm and optimism lead investors to concentrate resources in ways that later prove unsustainable. During such periods, rising asset prices often reinforce the belief that certain investments are inherently safe or destined to produce extraordinary returns.

As more capital flows toward the same opportunities, valuations rise further. Higher prices attract additional investors, who in turn reinforce the belief that the trend itself confirms underlying value. The cycle strengthens not only because capital is available, but also because the allocation process itself begins to amplify confidence.

Eventually, economic reality reasserts itself.

When expectations collapse, capital withdraws rapidly from the sectors that previously attracted enormous investment. Asset prices decline. Financial institutions experience losses. Economic activity slows as confidence disappears.

What had appeared to be a strong concentration of opportunity turns out to be a concentration of fragility.

These cycles reveal how sensitive financial systems can be to the quality of allocation decisions. Capital amplifies both sound judgment and collective error.

That truth is essential to understanding why allocation carries such weight. Capital is not neutral simply because it moves. Capital becomes consequential because its movement reinforces some structures while weakening others. The same force that can finance productive enterprise can also inflate speculation. The same system that can support durable institutions can also intensify instability when guided by distorted signals.

The consequences of allocation rarely remain confined to financial markets. They affect employment patterns, infrastructure development, technological progress, and the opportunities available within entire communities.

When capital is directed toward productive enterprise, toward innovation, infrastructure, and businesses that expand economic capability, societies often experience rising prosperity and broader opportunity.

When capital flows primarily toward speculation detached from productive activity, instability may begin accumulating beneath the surface of the financial system.

In modern economies, the authority to allocate capital frequently resides within institutions. Pension funds invest the retirement savings of millions of workers. Asset managers construct portfolios for households, foundations, endowments, and governments. Sovereign wealth funds deploy national resources across global markets. Venture capital firms finance early-stage companies whose technologies may reshape entire industries. Private equity firms determine which businesses gain the capital required for expansion or restructuring.

Collectively, these institutions control resources that can influence the direction of global economic development.

Yet the influence they exert is rarely visible to the public. Most people encounter financial systems indirectly through retirement accounts, employment opportunities, mortgages, household costs, or the broader economic conditions affecting their communities. The mechanisms guiding capital through the economy operate largely out of public view. Investment committees rarely make headlines, and asset allocation frameworks seldom appear outside professional circles.

Nevertheless, their consequences appear everywhere.

Cities grow where capital flows. Industries emerge where investors see potential. Technologies progress when resources enable innovation. Infrastructure improves where financing remains available long enough to support long-horizon projects. Entire regions can be transformed through sustained investment, while others fall behind when capital determines their prospects are less attractive.

Those guiding these decisions, therefore, occupy positions of unusual responsibility.

Their judgments determine which opportunities receive the resources required to grow and which remain unrealized.

Whether they fully recognize it or not, their decisions influence the economic environment that future generations will inherit.

Power is often associated with political authority. Governments pass laws, collect taxes, and regulate societal behavior. These forms of influence are visible and widely discussed. Yet capital allocation represents another form of power that often operates more quietly and with far less public scrutiny.

Those who direct capital shape the structure of economies by determining which industries receive investment, which technologies advance, and which communities gain access to financial resources.

In many cases, this influence extends far beyond national borders. Global investment flows determine where manufacturing capacity is built, which energy systems expand, which transportation corridors are financed, and which emerging markets gain access to the capital required for development.

A decision made within a pension system, family office, sovereign fund, or large asset management firm can influence outcomes in regions far removed from the institution that made it.

Capital, therefore, functions as one of the primary organizing forces within the global economy. It channels resources toward certain paths while leaving others unexplored. It rewards some assumptions and deprives others of support. Over time, repeated patterns of allocation gradually shape the architecture of economic life.

This is why the power of allocation matters so deeply.

Its significance does not arise from the mere existence of financial resources. It arises from the consequences that follow from their direction.

Every allocation decision reflects a judgment about the future.

Investors determine which ideas deserve support, which enterprises merit expansion, and which institutions receive the resources necessary to endure. These decisions rarely appear dramatic when they occur. But over time, they accumulate. They shape industries, influence technological development, reinforce incentives, and determine the economic possibilities available to entire societies.

Capital may appear abstract when viewed through financial statements and market indices, but the outcomes of allocation are anything but abstract. They are visible in the infrastructure societies build, the technologies they develop the institutions they sustain, and the communities they either strengthen or neglect.

At this point, an important distinction begins to emerge.

There is a difference between moving capital and directing it well.

A system can be highly efficient in moving money while remaining careless about what those flows reinforce over time. It can reward speed without supporting durability. It can generate returns while quietly weakening the structures upon which those returns ultimately depend.

This is why the power of allocation cannot be understood purely in terms of performance. It must also be understood in terms of consequence.

This is where the idea of stewardship begins to enter the conversation more fully.

If allocation determines what becomes possible, then those entrusted with directing capital carry a responsibility that extends beyond immediate return. They are not merely arranging portfolios. They are participating in decisions that shape economies and the durability of institutions. Their work affects not only markets but the broader systems through which people live, build, save, work, and plan for the future.

That responsibility does not eliminate the need for discipline, performance, or rigorous analysis.

It deepens the meaning of them.

Because the true question is not simply whether capital has been allocated efficiently.

The deeper question is whether it has been allocated wisely.

Wisdom in this context does not mean sentimentality. It means recognizing that capital is never only financial. It carries the accumulated effort of workers, families, institutions, and societies. When those resources are directed, their effects extend outward through systems, potentially enduring for years, decades, or generations.

Capital determines what becomes possible. Allocation determines where capital goes. And once capital begins moving in consistent directions across financial systems, those patterns begin shaping the structure of the world itself.

The chapters that follow will continue exploring how this process unfolds, how incentives shape these decisions, and how systems drift when stewardship is absent.

But at the center of the matter lies a simple truth.

The power of capital is not found merely in its possession.

It is found in its direction.

And the direction of capital is never a small thing.

Part II

Systems and Power

"It is difficult to get a man to understand something,
when his salary depends
upon his not understanding it."

Upton Sinclair
I, Candidate for Governor: And How I Got Licked

Chapter 4

Incentives Shape Systems

Financial systems are often described as if they were machines. Market commentary treats "the market" as a single entity that absorbs information, evaluates risk, and produces outcomes with mechanical precision. Charts rise and fall. Interest rates adjust. Capital moves across industries and regions in patterns that appear to follow a rational and almost automatic economic logic. From a distance, the system can look impersonal, as if financial markets operate according to rules as fixed and predictable as the laws of physics.

But financial systems are not machines. They are human systems.

Behind every investment decision, every capital allocation, and every capital movement lies a network of individuals responding to incentives. Portfolio managers evaluate opportunities within the constraints of their mandates. Executives attempt to grow companies while maintaining investor confidence. Institutional investors balance long-term obligations against short-term performance expectations. Analysts interpret data while also trying to preserve credibility with clients, colleagues, and markets. Each participant operates within a framework that shapes decision-making.

From the vantage point of any one individual, those decisions often appear rational. A portfolio manager may pursue a strategy designed to protect client capital while remaining competitive with peers. An executive may prioritize quarterly performance because public markets evaluate companies through that lens. A trader may seek opportunities that can produce strong returns within the period used to measure success. Viewed individually, these choices can seem disciplined, even necessary.

Collectively, however, they shape the behavior of the entire system.

This distinction matters because incentives ultimately determine how capital moves through the economy. When incentives reward patience and long-horizon thinking, capital tends to flow toward investments capable of producing durable value. Infrastructure projects, research initiatives, and enterprises that require years of development become viable when investors are willing to support them over extended periods. When incentives emphasize immediate performance, however, capital begins moving differently. Strategies that produce rapid returns attract attention. Opportunities that appear profitable in the short term receive increasing support. Investments whose benefits unfold slowly may struggle to attract resources, even when their long-term potential is substantial.

Financial systems, therefore, do not simply reflect economic reality. They respond to the incentives embedded within the institutions that operate them.

Understanding this helps explain why certain patterns recur throughout financial history. Periods of expansion often begin with a genuine opportunity. New technologies emerge. Productivity rises. Economic conditions support innovation and investment. Capital flows toward industries that appear capable of producing meaningful growth because investors recognize the potential for long-term return.

As these developments succeed, confidence grows. Early success attracts additional capital. Competition intensifies among institutions seeking to participate in rising markets. Asset managers begin comparing their performance against peers already benefiting from these gains. Executives work to demonstrate continued momentum to maintain investor enthusiasm. Financial professionals throughout the system observe these developments and adapt their strategies accordingly.

Gradually, the incentive structure begins to shift. At first, the change is subtle. Investors continue to support productive enterprises, but the pressure to match others' success grows. Managers who lag behind rising markets risk losing clients. Analysts whose forecasts appear overly cautious may lose credibility in environments increasingly shaped by optimism. As John C. Bogle observed, "The stock market is a giant distraction to the business of investing." The observation is not a rejection of markets, but a recognition of how easily attention shifts from long-term capital allocation to short-term price movement.

As incentives tilt toward short-term outcomes, the system's collective behavior begins to change. Capital flows more rapidly toward opportunities promising immediate gains. Strategies that produce rapid returns attract attention, while investments whose benefits unfold over longer horizons struggle to compete for resources. What appears, at the level of the individual, to be rational adaptation gradually becomes, at the level of the system, a shift in priorities.

Over time, the system adapts to those incentives. Financial institutions design products that can attract capital quickly, sometimes emphasizing market appeal over long-term resilience. Analysts and rating agencies may reinforce prevailing optimism because challenging widely held assumptions carries professional risk. Institutions that might privately recognize growing vulnerabilities can still find themselves caught in the same pattern because deviating too far from consensus can lead to immediate consequences.

None of this requires recklessness or bad intentions. It emerges naturally from incentive structures.

The individuals working inside these systems are often thoughtful, intelligent, and acutely aware of the responsibilities they carry. Many recognize that risks may be developing beneath the surface. Yet they also understand that resisting prevailing strategies can carry a high professional cost. A portfolio manager who avoids a rapidly rising market may ultimately protect capital from future losses. But if that caution results in short-term underperformance relative to competitors, clients may withdraw assets long before the decision's wisdom becomes apparent. A manager who consistently resists prevailing trends may be judged not as prudent but as ineffective.

A similar dynamic affects corporate leadership. Executives running publicly traded companies operate within systems that reward quarterly earnings growth and visible momentum. Even when leadership teams understand the long-term value of strategic investment, they must still consider how markets will react to temporary declines in profitability. Investors focused on immediate results may interpret those decisions as a sign of weakness rather than foresight. The result is a subtle but powerful pressure toward immediate outcomes, even when long-term thinking would produce greater durability.

These dynamics are not unique to finance. Incentive structures shape behavior across nearly every complex organization. What makes financial systems particularly sensitive to them is the speed at which capital can move. Modern markets allow enormous quantities of capital to shift across sectors, asset classes, and geographic regions within moments. When incentives encourage investors to pursue certain strategies, capital can move rapidly in that direction. This speed amplifies both opportunity and risk.

One of the clearest examples is the role of performance benchmarks. Institutional investors frequently evaluate asset managers relative to indices such as the S&P 500 and other widely followed benchmarks. These comparisons are intended to help clients determine whether managers are adding value through active decision making. In principle, benchmarks provide a useful reference point.

In practice, however, benchmarks also shape behavior.

Managers who fall significantly behind their benchmarks may face client withdrawals regardless of whether their strategy ultimately proves correct over a longer horizon. As a result, many managers feel pressure to remain closely aligned with the index itself, even when they believe certain assets may be overvalued. This dynamic can produce what is often described as herding. When large numbers of investors pursue similar strategies to avoid underperforming benchmarks, capital begins flowing into the same assets at the same time. Prices rise not solely because of underlying value, but because the incentive structure encourages participation.

Over time, the distinction between investing based on fundamental value and investing based on benchmark alignment can begin to blur. The system rewards those who remain close to prevailing trends and penalizes those who diverge too far from consensus. In this way, incentives can quietly reinforce cycles of expansion and contraction as capital concentrates in particular sectors, only to retreat rapidly when conditions change.

Compensation structures introduce another powerful layer of influence. In many areas of finance, compensation is closely tied to short-term performance metrics. Bonuses may be calculated on annual or even quarterly results. Professionals who generate strong returns within those windows may receive substantial rewards, while those pursuing strategies that require longer horizons may struggle to demonstrate success within the same evaluative frame.

Again, this behavior is rarely malicious. Professionals respond rationally to the incentives placed before them. When compensation rewards short-term performance, rational actors will naturally seek opportunities that yield strong short-term results.

Over longer horizons, however, these incentives can accumulate unintended consequences. Strategies designed to maximize immediate gains may introduce vulnerabilities that remain hidden during favorable market conditions. As long as asset prices continue rising, those vulnerabilities may appear manageable or even invisible. When conditions shift, however, the fragility embedded within the system can become visible very quickly.

Financial history offers repeated examples of this pattern. Institutions pursue strategies that appear profitable within the prevailing incentive framework, only to discover later that the risks embedded within those strategies were far greater than anticipated. When many institutions simultaneously follow similar incentives, the resulting instability can extend far beyond any individual organization.

Again, the global financial crisis of 2008 remains one of the clearest illustrations of how these dynamics can operate across multiple layers of the financial system. Mortgage originators were rewarded for generating new loans. Investment banks structured securities designed to distribute those loans across global markets. Rating agencies assessed these securities using models that typically presumed housing prices would stay fairly steady. Institutional investors purchased these instruments in pursuit of yields that appeared attractive relative to other available assets.

Each participant could explain their actions within a seemingly rational framework. Yet collectively, these incentives directed enormous volumes of capital toward structures whose risks were not fully understood. The system appeared to function smoothly as long as housing prices continued rising. When that assumption failed, the fragility embedded within the structure became visible across the global financial system.

The lesson from episodes like this is not that incentives should be eliminated. Incentives are necessary. They motivate effort, reward innovation, and coordinate activity across complex markets. The challenge lies in designing incentive structures that better align individual behavior with long-term system stability.

When incentives reward decisions that strengthen resilience over time, financial systems become more durable. Institutions allocate capital toward investments capable of sustaining growth across economic cycles. Risk management becomes part of strategic decision-making rather than a secondary concern addressed only after periods of rapid expansion. Markets do not become perfect under these conditions, but they do become better aligned with the long-term responsibilities embedded in capital allocation.

Achieving this alignment is not easy. Complex financial systems inevitably contain competing priorities. Investors seek returns. Institutions compete for clients and market share. Economic conditions evolve unpredictably. No incentive framework can eliminate uncertainty or guarantee wise decisions in every circumstance.

What thoughtful incentive design can do, however, is influence the direction of behavior across the system.

Small changes in how performance is measured, how compensation is structured, and how institutions evaluate risk can gradually reshape the patterns of allocation that define financial markets. Over time, these adjustments can foster a culture less oriented toward short-term opportunism and more toward stewardship.

That shift begins with a simple recognition. Incentives are never neutral.

Every structure that rewards certain behaviors will discourage others. By examining the incentives embedded within financial institutions, it becomes possible to understand why capital flows the way it does and why particular patterns repeat across decades of market history. Allocation determines the direction of capital. Incentives determine how those decisions are made.

Understanding this relationship reveals a deeper truth about financial systems. The stability of markets does not depend solely on regulations, models, or technological infrastructure. It depends on the motivations, shaping the judgments of the people operating within them. When incentives encourage careful stewardship of capital, markets can support long-term economic progress. When incentives prioritize immediate outcomes without regard for systemic consequence, the seeds of future instability may already be taking root.

Recognizing this dynamic is essential for anyone seeking to understand how financial systems actually operate. Because once it becomes clear how incentives shape behavior, another question follows almost immediately.

What happens when those incentives begin pushing the entire system in the wrong direction?

That question leads directly to the next stage of the story, the moment when systems begin to drift.

Chapter 5

When Systems Drift

Financial crises rarely arrive without warning. In retrospect, market collapses often appear sudden and dramatic. Prices fall rapidly, institutions fail, and systems that once seemed stable unravel in a matter of days or weeks. The speed of these events creates the impression that instability emerged unexpectedly, as though a shock had struck markets no one could have anticipated.

Yet the visible crisis is rarely the beginning of the story.

Long before panic appears on trading screens, financial systems begin changing in quieter ways. Structures evolve. Incentives shift. Strategies adapt to new conditions. Each adjustment appears minor in isolation, yet together they reshape the system over time. What eventually becomes visible as a crisis often begins as a slower, less dramatic process, a gradual movement away from the conditions that once supported stability.

This gradual transformation might be described as drift.

Drift does not occur because participants deliberately seek instability. On the contrary, most people operating within financial systems are trying to act responsibly within the rules, expectations, and incentives governing their environment. Institutions adapt to remain competitive. Investors pursue strategies that appear rational given the information available to them. Regulators revise frameworks in response to changing political, economic, or market conditions. Viewed individually, these decisions often appear reasonable.

Over time, however, those adjustments accumulate. The system begins to move away from the conditions that originally supported disciplined decision-making. What once served as a stable foundation slowly shifts until the distance between the system's original purpose and its current behavior becomes difficult to ignore. This is one of the central realities of modern finance. Instability often develops not through rupture at the outset, but through gradual deviation.

Financial systems are always evolving. New technologies change the speed at which information travels. Regulatory frameworks shift in response to politics, crises, and changing assumptions about markets. Institutions refine their strategies to compete within an environment that is never static. Much of this adaptation is useful. It allows financial systems to respond to new opportunities, absorb new information, and allocate capital more efficiently.

Adaptation is not the problem. The challenge arises when adaptation slowly becomes distortion.

The process often begins with incentives. As the previous chapter demonstrated, incentives shape how individuals and institutions behave within financial systems. They encourage certain outcomes while discouraging others. When incentives reward disciplined risk management and long-horizon thinking, institutions tend to reinforce patterns that support resilience. When incentives begin to favor short-term performance, however, the system's behavior can start to change in ways that are not immediately obvious.

The early stages of that change are rarely dramatic. An investment strategy that once appeared aggressive begins to look reasonable when competitors adopt similar approaches. Financial products designed to generate modest returns evolve into more complex instruments promising higher yields. Risk management frameworks adapt to accommodate these innovations, often on the assumption that markets have become more sophisticated, more liquid, or better at distributing risk. Each adjustment appears logical on its own.

Institutions compete for capital, and investors naturally gravitate toward opportunities offering stronger returns. As new strategies demonstrate success, they attract additional resources. Competitors respond by adopting similar approaches to remain relevant. Over time, practices that once existed at the edge of the market move toward the center. What was once unusual becomes familiar. What once required scrutiny begins to feel routine.

Slowly, the system's center of gravity begins to shift.

Strategies that once would have been approached cautiously become widely accepted. Risk tolerance increases, sometimes without participants fully recognizing how much conditions have changed. Financial models built on recent data reinforce the belief that the environment remains stable, even as the assumptions supporting that stability begin to weaken beneath the surface. Drift often becomes visible only in retrospect because it rarely announces itself while it is happening.

Leverage offers one of the clearest illustrations of this process. Used carefully, leverage can support productive investment, increase flexibility, and improve liquidity within markets. Businesses often rely on borrowed capital to expand operations or finance large projects that would otherwise be difficult to undertake. Within limits, leverage can serve legitimate and even constructive purposes.

Yet leverage also magnifies loss.

During periods of expansion, the risks associated with leverage can appear manageable. Rising asset prices create a cushion against declines, and institutions develop increasingly sophisticated tools to measure exposure. As confidence grows, investors gradually increase leverage to pursue higher returns. At first, these increases appear modest. Each decision seems justified by prevailing conditions, recent performance, or the apparent success of peers.

As more institutions adopt similar strategies, however, the system's overall sensitivity begins to rise. Each decision may appear prudent within its immediate context, yet collectively the system becomes more vulnerable to changes in asset prices. That vulnerability may remain hidden for years. Only when markets begin moving in unexpected ways does the accumulated leverage reveal itself. Institutions facing losses may be forced to reduce positions simultaneously. As they attempt to sell assets to reduce exposure, prices decline further, triggering additional selling.

What once appeared stable can quickly become unstable. What once appeared strong can suddenly reveal itself to be fragile.

This pattern reflects the deeper mechanics of systemic drift. As incentives favor strategies that generate immediate gains, institutions may gradually prioritize opportunities offering short-term returns without fully accounting for long-term consequences. Financial innovations originally designed to improve efficiency can evolve into structures whose complexity obscures the risks they contain. Participants within the system may recognize some of these developments yet still feel constrained by the same incentives that influence everyone else.

A fund manager who reduces exposure to a rapidly rising asset class may protect capital over the long run but can also risk losing clients who expect competitive short-term performance. A financial institution that declines to participate in profitable but increasingly complex transactions may watch competitors gain market share. Even regulators may struggle to respond when innovation moves faster than the frameworks designed to govern it. The result is a powerful gravitational pull within the system.

Institutions begin moving in similar directions not because all participants share identical beliefs, but because the incentive structures surrounding them reward similar behavior. Diverging too far from prevailing strategies can carry professional, commercial, or institutional costs. Over time, this leads to gradual convergence in behavior. Capital flows toward similar opportunities. Investment strategies become increasingly correlated. The diversity of judgment and approach that once helped create resilience begins to narrow.

What once looked like a competitive ecosystem of independent actors is now behaving more like a system operating in parallel.

When many participants pursue similar strategies simultaneously, vulnerability increases. The illusion of stability can persist for long periods. Rising asset prices reinforce confidence. The absence of recent crises supports the belief that the system is more resilient than it was in the past. Sophisticated models, rating frameworks, and technological infrastructure can further reinforce the impression that risk is being carefully managed.

In reality, the opposite may be occurring.

Complex structures can conceal vulnerabilities that remain dormant until conditions change. Interconnected markets transmit shocks rapidly, allowing disturbances in one sector to spread across others. Institutions relying on similar models and assumptions may respond to unexpected events in nearly identical ways. Under these conditions, even modest disruptions can cascade through the system with surprising speed.

Financial history offers repeated examples of this pattern. In many cases, participants believed they were operating within rational frameworks supported by advanced analytical tools. The gradual evolution of strategies, structures, and incentives made it difficult to recognize how much the system had changed. Only after a crisis occurred did observers begin tracing the path that led there.

In retrospect, warning signs were often evident long before the collapse. Leverage had increased steadily. Asset valuations had moved away from underlying fundamentals. Financial structures had grown more complex than the institutions managing them fully understood. None of these developments appeared catastrophic on its own. Together, however, they reflected a system drifting away from its original foundations.

This is one of the most important truths about financial instability. Crises rarely emerge from a single catastrophic decision. More often, they develop through the accumulation of smaller choices that gradually reshape the system's structure. Each choice appears reasonable within its immediate context, yet collectively those choices alter the environment in which future decisions are made. The drift becomes embedded in the system before the crisis becomes visible on the surface.

Recognizing drift, therefore, requires perspective.

Participants deeply embedded within financial systems often struggle to see the broader trajectory of change. Daily responsibilities focus attention on immediate challenges. Portfolio managers monitor positions. Executives respond to investors. Analysts revise forecasts. Regulators address emerging issues one at a time. Within that cadence, there is often little space to step back and ask whether the structure itself is changing in ways that matter.

This is one reason long periods of apparent stability can coexist with the gradual accumulation of systemic risk. By the time vulnerabilities become widely visible, the forces driving drift may already be deeply embedded in the system's architecture.

For institutions responsible for allocating capital, the challenge is therefore not limited to managing risk inside existing frameworks. It also requires awareness of how those frameworks themselves may be changing over time. Stewardship demands this wider field of vision. Those entrusted with directing capital must occasionally step back from the immediacy of markets and ask whether the structures guiding their decisions still support the stability they were originally designed to protect. They must ask whether incentives, strategies, and institutional norms remain aligned with the longer-term responsibilities embedded in capital allocation.

When systems drift too far from those foundations, the consequences rarely remain confined to financial markets. They affect employment, economic growth, institutional confidence, and the broader stability upon which communities depend. The weight of capital becomes visible not only in asset prices but in the lives altered when financial instability spreads outward into the real economy.

Understanding this process is essential for anyone seeking to understand how crises develop. But it also raises a deeper question. If systems drift gradually through the accumulation of seemingly rational decisions, how can participants recognize that drift before instability becomes undeniable?

Because even when drift remains invisible to many, financial systems often begin sending signals that something beneath the surface has changed.

The challenge is learning how to recognize them.

Chapter 6

The Early Warning Signs

As previously stated, financial crises often appear sudden. Markets fall rapidly. Institutions fail. Systems that once seemed stable unravel within days or weeks. By the time disruption becomes visible, the collapse can feel abrupt and unpredictable, as though a stable structure has suddenly lost its balance.

Yet instability rarely emerges without warning.

As discussed, financial systems tend to drift gradually over time. Incentives shift, strategies evolve, and risk tolerance slowly increases. Each adjustment appears reasonable when viewed in isolation, but collectively these changes reshape the system's underlying structure. By the time instability becomes visible, the forces driving it may have been building quietly for years.

Drift, however, rarely occurs in silence.

Long before a crisis becomes obvious, financial systems begin displaying signals that something beneath the surface has changed. These signals rarely arrive as dramatic alarms. More often, they emerge through patterns that reveal how capital is behaving across the system. For those willing to observe, markets often provide clues that the relationship between confidence and reality is beginning to change.

Recognizing those patterns is one of the most important responsibilities of anyone entrusted with allocating capital. Crises may be unpredictable in their precise timing, but the conditions that make them possible often develop slowly and visibly. Stewardship does not require predicting the exact day of the market break. It requires developing the discipline to recognize when stability may be more fragile than it appears.

One of the earliest warning signs is when asset prices begin to drift away from the economic fundamentals that support them. During healthy periods of expansion, valuations tend to rise alongside improvements in productivity, earnings, and economic growth. Companies generate higher profits. Industries expand. New technologies improve efficiency or open entirely new markets. Under such conditions, it is reasonable for investors to assign greater value to assets associated with those developments.

Over time, however, enthusiasm can begin moving faster than the underlying reality. Prices rise not only because present conditions are improving, but because expectations of future growth become increasingly ambitious. Investors justify higher valuations by pointing to innovation, structural change, or new sources of productivity. Markets reward those who identify emerging opportunities early, and rising prices appear to confirm that the optimism is justified.

At this stage, the distinction between disciplined foresight and expanding speculation can become difficult to see.

As prices continue to rise, narratives often replace analysis. Expectations of future appreciation gradually become more influential than the present financial reality. Capital begins flowing toward momentum rather than underlying value. The market starts rewarding participation in a rising trend more than careful assessment of the asset itself.

This pattern has appeared repeatedly throughout financial history. In the late 1920s, enthusiasm for technologies such as radio and aviation helped push stock valuations to extraordinary levels. During the late 1990s, the rapid expansion of internet companies produced a similar wave of optimism. In both periods, investors believed they were witnessing the arrival of transformative economic eras. In important ways, they were right. Real innovation was taking place, and the world was changing.

But technological transformation does not eliminate financial gravity.

Eventually, the gap between expectations and economic reality becomes wider. When valuations depend too heavily on continued optimism, even modest disappointments can trigger rapid reassessments. The issue is not that innovation is unreal. The issue is that capital may begin pricing perfection long before reality can support it.

A second warning sign often emerges through the quiet expansion of leverage. Borrowed capital allows investors and institutions to increase the size of their positions, amplifying returns during favorable conditions. Used prudently, leverage can support productive investment and improve liquidity. Businesses often rely on borrowed capital to expand operations, finance infrastructure, or support innovation that might otherwise take far longer to develop.

Yet leverage magnifies losses just as effectively as it magnifies gains.

During periods of sustained growth, the risks associated with borrowing often appear manageable. Rising asset prices create a cushion against losses, and institutions develop increasingly sophisticated tools for measuring exposure. Confidence grows. Financing becomes more readily available. Gradually, leverage increases throughout the system.

Each increase may appear modest when viewed in isolation. Collectively, however, the system becomes more sensitive to changes in asset prices. When leverage is expanded across many institutions simultaneously, even relatively small market disruptions can trigger forced adjustments. As positions are reduced to contain losses, selling pressure accelerates price declines and spreads instability across markets.

The danger of leverage is not simply its size. It is the way it can remain hidden during periods when everything appears stable. As long as asset prices continue to rise and financing remains available, the system can exhibit far greater sensitivity than participants recognize. The vulnerability does not disappear. It waits.

Another important signal appears in the pricing of risk itself. During stable periods, investors demand compensation for uncertainty. Credit spreads widen to reflect the possibility of default. Risk premiums compensate investors for the unpredictability of markets, business conditions, or economic shocks. When conditions improve, those spreads often narrow for legitimate reasons.

But during extended expansions, the price of risk can fall too far.

Borrowing costs decline. Credit spreads compress. Investors become increasingly willing to accept lower compensation in exchange for greater uncertainty. This may reflect genuine improvement in economic conditions, but it can also reveal growing complacency. When market participants begin behaving as if uncertainty has largely disappeared, the system may drift into a more dangerous form of confidence.

When risk appears inexpensive, institutions naturally begin taking more of it. This is one of the recurring patterns observed in financial history. When the cost of caution feels high and the cost of risk feels low, the system encourages greater exposure. Institutions borrow more easily, investors accept lower premiums, and capital chases opportunities that appear safe precisely because recent stability has made them feel familiar.

Another indication arises when there is a perception of excess liquidity. During periods of optimism, financial markets often appear highly liquid. Buyers and sellers transact easily, and assets can be traded quickly without significant price movement. Participants begin assuming that liquidity will remain available whenever they need it. That assumption becomes embedded in portfolio construction, risk management, and institutional behavior.

In reality, liquidity in financial markets is not constant. It is a function of confidence.

When participants believe markets are stable, they are willing to provide capital and absorb risk. When confidence deteriorates, that willingness can disappear rapidly. Markets that once felt deep and flexible can become thin and unstable when many participants attempt to move at the same time.

This is one of the great paradoxes of financial systems. Periods preceding crises often feature markets that appear most liquid precisely when they are becoming structurally fragile. Investors assume they can easily exit positions if conditions change, yet when many participants attempt to reduce exposure simultaneously, liquidity can vanish almost instantly.

What once appeared stable can reveal itself as fragile.

The structure of investment strategies within the system can also provide early clues. Healthy financial markets benefit from diversity of approach. Different investors pursue opportunities using different time horizons, risk tolerances, and analytical frameworks. That diversity allows markets to absorb shocks because participants respond to changing conditions in varied ways.

As drift develops, however, this diversity often narrows. Strategies that deliver strong short-term performance attract increasing capital. Institutions adopt similar approaches to remain competitive. Over time, large portions of the financial system become exposed to the same assets, the same assumptions, and often the same models. What appears to be diversification gradually becomes concentration.

Concentrated allocation leads to fragility within financial systems.

When many institutions hold similar positions, even modest changes in market conditions can prompt simultaneous adjustments. Those adjustments amplify volatility, transforming what might have remained a localized disruption into broader instability. Markets become more vulnerable not simply because of the assets held, but because too many participants hold them for similar reasons and may respond similarly.

Perhaps the most deceptive warning sign of all is the apparent disappearance of risk itself. Periods preceding financial crises are often characterized by declining volatility and steady market performance. Price fluctuations diminish.

Credit spreads narrow. Risk models suggest that markets have become increasingly stable. The absence of disruption begins to reinforce the belief that the system is more resilient than it once was.

This calm environment can be deeply misleading.

Declining volatility does not always mean that risk has diminished. Sometimes it means risk has become hidden. When participants rely on similar assumptions and respond to conditions in synchronized ways, volatility can remain low until a disruption forces large numbers of institutions to reposition simultaneously. When that adjustment begins, volatility can return with remarkable speed.

The system does not become fragile when volatility reappears. It becomes visible.

Changes in the language surrounding financial markets can also provide important clues. As optimism grows, narratives begin dominating investment discussions. Certain industries or technologies are described as transformative, which seems to justify increasingly ambitious projections. New economic paradigms are declared. Traditional valuation frameworks are dismissed as outdated. Concepts that once invited scrutiny begin receiving near-automatic approval because they appear connected to the future.

Stories become easier to believe when recent performance appears to validate them. And that is precisely what makes them so powerful.

Narratives are not inherently false. In many cases, they emerge from genuine change. The danger lies in the way stories can make investors and the industry more willing to suspend discipline. When a narrative becomes strong enough, it can persuade investors to believe that ordinary constraints no longer apply. At that point, the market may begin rewarding belief more than judgment.

Yet narratives do not eliminate risk. More often, they make it easier to overlook.

These signals indicate vulnerability, not certainty. Financial systems are complex, and markets can remain resilient for extended periods even when vulnerabilities are present. Valuations may remain elevated longer than expected. Leverage may expand without immediate consequences. Innovation may genuinely justify higher expectations. Liquidity may remain available far longer than risk models suggest.

The purpose of identifying early warning signs is not to predict the exact timing of disruption. It is to recognize when the system's structure is changing.

Periods of drift are often characterized by the simultaneous appearance of several signals: rising valuations, expanding leverage, narrowing strategy diversity, compressed risk premiums, abundant liquidity, and growing reliance on optimistic narratives. Individually, these developments may appear manageable. Together, they suggest that the system may be becoming more fragile than it appears.

Recognizing these patterns requires perspective. Participants deeply embedded within financial markets often focus on immediate performance pressures and competitive dynamics. The signals of systemic drift may be visible yet difficult to acknowledge while markets continue to produce strong results. In such environments, caution can feel costly, and discipline can feel isolating.

For institutions responsible for allocating capital, this creates a difficult but essential challenge. Remaining disciplined during periods of optimism often requires resisting the very forces driving market expansion. It requires asking uncomfortable questions about valuations, leverage, liquidity, and the sustainability of prevailing strategies. It requires the willingness to look beyond what markets are rewarding in the present and consider what those rewards may be encouraging beneath the surface.

Those questions rarely produce easy answers. Yet they are indispensable for anyone seeking to understand how financial systems evolve. Crises may appear suddenly, but the forces that create them rarely do. They develop gradually through the accumulation of decisions, incentives, and expectations that reshape the system's structure.

This is where stewardship becomes more than an abstract principle.

A steward of capital does not wait for a crisis to confirm what could have been observed earlier. A steward learns to recognize the signals that suggest confidence is beginning to outrun reality. This does not mean withdrawing from all risk or attempting to eliminate uncertainty. It means understanding that financial stability is often most vulnerable at the very moments when markets appear most comfortable.

The discipline to recognize early warning signs does not eliminate risk. But it creates the possibility of responding before fragility hardens into a crisis. And that possibility matters, because once the warning signs become impossible to ignore, the system is usually much closer to disruption than it appears.

The question, then, is not whether markets send signals.

They do.

The deeper question is whether those entrusted with capital are willing to see them for what they are.

Chapter 7

The Psychology of Markets

By the time warning signs begin appearing in financial systems, another force has already been shaping events beneath the surface. It does not appear on balance sheets, nor can it be measured solely through leverage ratios, valuation metrics, or liquidity indicators. Yet it influences every one of those measures.

That force is human psychology.

Financial markets are often described as rational systems. Prices respond to information. Investors analyze data, assess risk, and allocate capital toward opportunities expected to generate the highest return. Economic theory frequently assumes that markets process information efficiently, allowing prices to reflect the collective judgment of participants acting in their own best interests.

There is truth in this framework. Markets do absorb enormous amounts of information. Millions of participants continuously evaluate economic developments, corporate performance, technological change, and geopolitical events. Over time, this decentralized process can direct capital toward productive enterprises and help societies allocate resources to support growth.

But financial markets are not purely analytical systems. They are systems populated by human beings.

Every decision made within financial markets, every trade, investment allocation, and lending judgment, ultimately reflects human interpretation. Investors process information through experience, institutional constraints, professional pressures, and emotional responses that shape how they perceive opportunity and risk. Even the most sophisticated financial models depend on assumptions constructed by people attempting to understand an uncertain future.

The result is a system in which psychology quietly but powerfully influences the movement of capital.

Economic fundamentals certainly matter. Productivity, earnings, innovation, and demographic trends all shape the long-term trajectory of markets. Yet those fundamentals do not operate in isolation. Periods of expansion and contraction are often accompanied by waves of confidence and doubt that move through the investment community. These waves influence how information is interpreted, how institutions deploy capital, and how quickly sentiment can shift when conditions change.

Understanding this psychological dimension is essential for anyone seeking to understand how markets actually behave.

One of the most consistent features of market psychology is the gradual rise of optimism during periods of success. When asset prices rise steadily over time, investors often interpret those gains as confirmation that their strategies are sound. Positive outcomes reinforce confidence, encouraging individuals and institutions to believe that favorable conditions may persist longer than history would normally suggest.

This response is not unique to finance. In nearly every field of human endeavor, success shapes perception. When actions produce favorable results, people naturally become more confident in the judgments that led to them.

Within financial markets, however, this feedback loop can become especially powerful.

Rising asset prices attract additional capital. Investors who initially hesitated may enter the market after observing sustained gains among their peers. Institutions responsible for managing large pools of capital begin allocating more resources toward strategies that appear successful. Performance becomes both validation and invitation.

Gradually, optimism spreads throughout the system.

What begins as confidence in specific investments often evolves into broader narratives that explain why the present moment marks a new era of opportunity. Technological innovation, structural economic change, or improved financial sophistication are cited as reasons the current environment differs fundamentally from the past.

These narratives often contain genuine insight. Periods of innovation do occur, and transformative technologies can reshape economies in ways that justify substantial investment. Railroads, electrification, aviation, the internet, and artificial intelligence all represent real economic transformations.

The challenge arises when optimism begins to separate from the discipline that originally justified it.

As confidence expands, investors may begin extrapolating recent success indefinitely into the future. Expectations for continued growth become embedded in asset prices. The margin for disappointment narrows as valuations reflect not only current conditions but also increasingly optimistic projections of what may come next.

At that stage, psychology begins influencing markets more strongly than underlying economic fundamentals.

Investors no longer evaluate opportunities solely according to intrinsic value. Increasingly, they evaluate opportunities relative to prevailing sentiment. Assets that attract attention begin drawing even more attention. Capital flows toward sectors that appear to be winning, while less fashionable opportunities struggle to attract investment regardless of their underlying potential.

Momentum gradually becomes a substitute for analysis.

Financial history offers many examples of this process. During the technology boom of the late 1990s, investor enthusiasm for the emerging internet economy led to extraordinary valuations for companies that had yet to generate meaningful revenue. The promise of technological transformation was genuine. The internet would go on to reshape global communication, commerce, and information exchange in ways few could have fully anticipated.

Yet during that period, capital flowed toward nearly any company associated with the emerging digital economy. Businesses with little more than a website and an ambitious vision raised enormous sums from investors eager to participate in what appeared to be a revolutionary moment. Traditional valuation frameworks were often dismissed as outdated. New metrics emerged to justify prevailing optimism, and early success stories reinforced the belief that the transformation underway warranted the extraordinary valuations being assigned to technology companies.

For a time, the momentum appeared unstoppable.

Capital poured into technology ventures, equity markets surged, and the success of early investors reinforced the belief that participation itself had become the primary source of opportunity.

Eventually, however, economic gravity reasserted itself.

When expected growth failed to materialize at the pace investors had assumed, confidence deteriorated rapidly. Capital that had once flowed freely into technology companies began retreating. Valuations collapsed across much of the sector, wiping out enormous sums of investor capital.

The technological transformation did not disappear. The internet still reshaped the global economy in profound ways. But the psychological cycle surrounding it changed dramatically. The lesson was not that the underlying innovation had been false. It was that psychology had encouraged capital to outrun the pace at which reality could justify expectation.

Market psychology, however, does not operate only during periods of expansion. It plays an equally powerful role during periods of decline.

Just as optimism can amplify upward movements in asset prices, fear can accelerate declines once uncertainty enters the system. Investors experiencing losses may begin reducing exposure to protect remaining capital. Institutions responsible for safeguarding client assets may face pressure to demonstrate that risks are being actively managed. These responses are understandable. Protecting capital during uncertain conditions is a rational objective.

Yet when many participants attempt to reduce exposure simultaneously, the resulting selling pressure can drive prices downward far more rapidly than underlying economic conditions alone would justify. Declines that begin gradually can accelerate quickly as sentiment shifts across the market.

Fear spreads through many of the same channels as optimism.

As prices fall, additional investors become concerned about potential losses. Narratives that once supported confidence begin shifting toward instability and risk. News events that might previously have been interpreted as temporary setbacks now appear to confirm that conditions are deteriorating.

Psychology reinforces the downward momentum.

The global financial crisis of 2008 demonstrated how rapidly confidence can collapse when uncertainty arises about the stability of financial institutions. As uncertainty spread across the financial system, investors withdrew capital at an accelerating pace. Credit markets froze, liquidity evaporated, and asset prices declined across multiple sectors simultaneously.

The speed of the decline reflected more than economic deterioration. It reflected the sudden collapse of confidence.

Modern financial systems amplify these psychological dynamics because information now travels almost instantly across global networks. News affecting one region or sector can influence sentiment worldwide within minutes. Investors respond not only to economic data but also to reactions from other participants. The market becomes a system in which people are constantly interpreting both reality and one another.

This creates powerful feedback loops.

When prices rise, confidence increases and attracts additional capital. When prices fall, fear spreads, encouraging further selling. In both directions, psychological responses amplify the underlying movement of markets.

Institutional structures can intensify these effects. Many investment professionals operate within environments that reward short-term performance. Portfolio managers are evaluated quarterly or annually. Asset management firms compete for capital based on relative returns measured over limited horizons. These structures influence behavior even when individuals understand the longer-term risks associated with prevailing strategies.

During rising markets, remaining fully invested may feel like the safest professional decision. Underperforming peers during periods of expansion can carry meaningful career consequences. Conversely, during downturns, reducing exposure may appear prudent even when long-term valuations are beginning to look more attractive.

In this way, professional incentives and human psychology often reinforce one another.

Understanding market psychology, therefore, requires acknowledging a simple but profound reality. Financial markets are systems in which human beings attempt to make decisions about an uncertain future.

Investors rely on models, historical data, and institutional experience to guide their decisions. Yet uncertainty can never be eliminated. The future cannot be known with certainty, and every investment decision ultimately reflects a judgment about how present conditions may evolve.

Under such circumstances, psychological forces inevitably influence how risks and opportunities are interpreted.

Confidence and caution, optimism and fear, discipline and impatience all shape the allocation decisions that ultimately determine how capital moves through financial systems. Over long periods, economic fundamentals tend to reassert themselves, correcting distortions introduced by collective behavior. Within shorter periods, however, psychology can create significant deviations.

Investors may temporarily overestimate the potential of emerging opportunities or underestimate the risks embedded within complex financial structures. Those distortions are eventually corrected, but the correction process can produce severe volatility and substantial economic consequences.

For institutions responsible for allocating capital, recognizing the psychological dimension of markets is essential.

Effective capital allocation requires more than analytical skill. It requires awareness of how sentiment and perception influence behavior across the financial system. Institutions capable of maintaining discipline during periods of extreme optimism or fear are often better positioned to direct capital responsibly over long horizons.

This insight returns us to the book's broader theme. Capital allocation decisions occur within systems shaped not only by economic fundamentals but also by human motivation. Incentives influence behavior, and psychology influences how those incentives are interpreted. Together, these forces shape the patterns through which capital flows across the global economy.

Recognizing this dynamic leads to a deeper question.

If markets are influenced as much by human psychology as by economic reality, how reliable are the tools investors rely upon to measure and control risk?

And if those tools prove inadequate during moments of stress, who ultimately bears the consequences of the capital that has been deployed?

The answers to those questions begin revealing the deeper responsibility carried by those entrusted with directing capital.

And understanding that responsibility brings the framework closer to its center.

Chapter 8

The Illusion of Control

Modern finance is built upon an extraordinary confidence in measurement. Financial institutions track risk exposures to the smallest decimal point. Sophisticated models estimate potential losses across thousands of hypothetical market scenarios. Portfolio managers analyze correlations, volatility patterns, and macroeconomic indicators to understand how assets might behave under changing conditions. Entire departments exist within major financial organizations whose sole purpose is to quantify uncertainty as precisely as possible.

From the outside, the system appears remarkably exact. Risk can be expressed as a number. Portfolio outcomes can be simulated across countless possible futures. Institutions construct elaborate analytical frameworks designed to ensure that capital is deployed responsibly and that unexpected disruptions remain within acceptable limits. Within this architecture lies one of the defining convictions of modern finance, that uncertainty can be measured.

Financial institutions rely on analytical tools designed to translate unpredictable outcomes into measurable probabilities. Among the most widely used is Value at Risk, often referred to simply as VaR. This metric estimates the maximum expected loss a portfolio might incur over a specific time horizon under normal market conditions. A portfolio might report a daily VaR of $10 million at a 95% confidence level. In practical terms, this suggests that, under typical market conditions, the portfolio should not lose more than $10 million in a single day and no more than 5% of the time. Risk managers monitor exposures across trading desks, senior executives assess whether portfolios remain within acceptable limits, and regulators evaluate whether institutions are maintaining appropriate safeguards.

Measurements such as these provide a framework for decision-making. They offer a language through which risk can be discussed, compared, and governed. They allow institutions managing billions or even trillions of dollars to impose structure on an otherwise overwhelming level of complexity. In addition to these daily metrics, institutions rely heavily on stress testing to explore how portfolios might behave under extreme conditions. Analysts simulate historical disruptions, such as the 1987 market crash, the Asian financial crisis of the late 1990s, and the 2008 global financial crisis. By modeling how current portfolios might respond to similar events, institutions attempt to prepare for shocks that have not yet occurred.

These tools have improved financial decision-making in important ways. Quantitative modeling enables institutions to evaluate complex portfolios that would be impossible to assess solely through intuition. Advances in computing power allow analysts to simulate decades of historical market behavior in minutes. Risk managers can monitor exposures across entire organizations in real time, giving executives a degree of visibility that previous generations of financiers could scarcely imagine. The analytical capabilities of modern finance are remarkable.

Yet beneath this sophistication lies a more enduring challenge. Financial markets operate within an environment of genuine uncertainty.

No model can perfectly predict how economic conditions will evolve. No system of equations can anticipate how investors will respond to new information, how governments will react during political crises, or how technological change may reshape entire industries. Even the most advanced analytical frameworks cannot eliminate the fundamental uncertainty surrounding the future. They can describe possibilities. They can estimate probabilities. They can help institutions think more clearly. But they cannot convert the unknown into something fully controllable.

The tension between uncertainty and the desire for control lies at the heart of modern financial risk management. Institutions must attempt to manage risks they cannot fully predict. Investors expect portfolio managers to demonstrate discipline and foresight. Boards of directors demand that executives maintain stability while still pursuing growth. Regulators expect financial institutions to show that the risks embedded within their balance sheets remain manageable. To navigate this tension, financial systems rely heavily on models that translate uncertainty into probabilities.

By examining historical market behavior, analysts attempt to estimate how assets may perform under various conditions. These estimates guide decisions about how much capital to allocate to different investments and how much exposure an institution can reasonably tolerate. In theory, this provides a structured approach for managing the complexity of modern markets. In practice, however, it can introduce a subtle but powerful illusion.

When risk is expressed through carefully calculated metrics, it becomes tempting to believe that uncertainty has been reduced to something manageable.

Institutions may begin interpreting model outputs as evidence that their portfolios are protected against extreme outcomes, even though those models are built upon assumptions that may not hold in the future. The problem does not arise because models are inherently misguided. Many are mathematically rigorous and grounded in decades of empirical research. The danger lies not in models, but in mistaking their confidence for truth.

Models are representations of reality. They are not reality itself.

Every model relies on assumptions about how markets behave, how assets interact, and how investors respond to changing conditions. These assumptions may appear reasonable during stable periods. Yet they can break down quickly when markets move into unfamiliar territory. Financial history offers repeated examples of institutions discovering the limits of their models during periods of stress.

One of the most famous occurred in the late 1990s with the rise and fall of Long-Term Capital Management. The hedge fund was founded by some of the most respected figures in financial economics. Its leadership included Nobel Prize-winning economists and traders with decades of experience in global markets. The firm employed advanced mathematical models designed to identify small pricing discrepancies between related securities. These discrepancies often appeared between government bonds, derivatives, and other financial instruments that historically moved in predictable relationships with one another.

The strategy relied on convergence. If two securities that normally traded in close alignment temporarily diverged in price, the models predicted that those prices would eventually return to their historical relationship. By purchasing the undervalued security and shorting the overvalued one, the fund sought to profit when the relationship normalized. Because the pricing differences were often small, the strategy relied heavily on leverage. Borrowed capital allowed the fund to amplify its positions, turning minor pricing inefficiencies into substantial profits.

During its early years, the strategy appeared extraordinarily successful. Returns were robust, volatility was minimal, and the fund's trading models seemed dependable. Investors and counterparties grew confident in the fund's ability to manage risk through sophisticated analysis. Yet the models relied on assumptions about market behavior that proved fragile during periods of stress.

In 1998, a series of unexpected global events disrupted financial markets. Russia defaulted on its sovereign debt, triggering widespread uncertainty across global markets. Investors suddenly began reducing exposure to risky assets, causing price relationships between securities to diverge dramatically from historical norms. While the models' initial predictions appeared to converge, they ultimately diverged. Because the fund had employed significant leverage, these movements produced losses far larger than its risk metrics had anticipated.

Within weeks, Long-Term Capital Management faced collapse.

The episode shocked the financial world not only because of the scale of the losses, but because of who was involved. If some of the most sophisticated minds in financial economics could misjudge risk so dramatically, what did that suggest about the broader confidence financial systems had placed in their models? The lesson was not that quantitative analysis was useless. It was that there is danger in confusing a map with the terrain.

Financial systems are dynamic environments shaped by economic forces, political developments, technological change, and human behavior. Models constructed from historical data cannot fully anticipate how these forces may interact during unprecedented events. When institutions place excessive confidence in their models, they may become vulnerable to precisely the risks those models were designed to help them understand.

The illusion of control becomes especially powerful during periods of stability. When markets behave predictably, models appear to work exactly as intended. Risk estimates align with observed outcomes, reinforcing confidence in the analytical frameworks guiding investment decisions. Institutions may therefore increase exposure to strategies that appear well understood within the model's assumptions.

Over time, however, the system adapts.

As more participants adopt similar modeling approaches, their behavior becomes increasingly aligned. Institutions may hold similar positions, rely on similar risk metrics, and respond to market signals in comparable ways. What appears to be careful risk management at the individual level can produce unexpected consequences when repeated across the system as a whole.

This convergence creates hidden vulnerability. If many institutions attempt to reduce risk simultaneously in response to a model-generated signal, the resulting market movement can amplify volatility rather than contain it. Actions intended to stabilize individual portfolios may instead destabilize markets when large numbers of participants respond in similar ways at the same time.

The global financial crisis of 2008 revealed another dimension of this problem. Before the crisis, many financial institutions relied heavily on models to evaluate the risk of mortgage-backed securities. These models attempted to estimate the probability that borrowers would default on their mortgages and how those defaults might affect the performance of large loan pools. Because mortgages were bundled together from different geographic regions, the models assumed that risks were diversified. If homeowners in one region experienced financial difficulty, borrowers in other regions would continue making payments, protecting investors from widespread losses.

For years, these assumptions appeared reasonable. Housing prices rose steadily. Default rates remained relatively low. Mortgage-backed securities received high credit ratings, and financial institutions increased their exposure to these assets. The models appeared to be working.

Yet the models relied on a critical assumption, that housing markets across the United States would not decline simultaneously.

When housing prices began falling nationwide, that assumption collapsed. Borrowers across multiple regions began defaulting simultaneously. Mortgage-backed securities, once considered safe, suddenly experienced large losses. Institutions that believed they had carefully measured and controlled their risks discovered that the models guiding their decisions had failed to capture the true complexity of the housing market.

The illusion of control dissolved.

Episodes like these reveal an important principle about financial risk. Uncertainty cannot be eliminated. It can be studied, managed, and mitigated, but it cannot be reduced to a set of numbers that perfectly describe the future. Markets are influenced by events that lie beyond historical data. Political decisions, technological breakthroughs, natural disasters, and shifts in collective behavior all shape outcomes in ways models cannot fully anticipate.

Recognizing this limitation does not diminish the value of quantitative analysis. On the contrary, models remain essential tools for understanding complex financial systems. They provide structure for decision-making and help institutions identify risks that might otherwise go unnoticed. The challenge lies in maintaining humility about what models can achieve.

Institutions that treat models as guides rather than guarantees are better positioned to adapt when conditions change. Analytical frameworks must be complemented by judgment, experience, and awareness of the broader environment in which markets operate. Numbers can inform wisdom. They cannot replace it.

This perspective closely aligns with the concept of stewardship introduced earlier in the book. Stewardship requires acknowledging the limits of control. Those responsible for allocating capital must recognize that uncertainty is an inherent feature of financial systems. Rather than attempting to eliminate uncertainty, they must build strategies that remain resilient in the face of the unexpected.

Such resilience depends less on precise prediction than on thoughtful preparation. Diversification, prudent leverage, and careful attention to systemic risk can help institutions withstand shocks that models fail to anticipate. These practices reflect an understanding that financial systems are not static mechanisms, but evolving environments shaped by countless interacting forces.

As instruments, institutions, and global markets become increasingly interconnected, the ability of any single participant to grasp the whole system diminishes. Even well-designed models may struggle to capture the full range of interactions unfolding across modern financial networks.

This growing complexity introduces another challenge.

If uncertainty cannot be fully controlled and models cannot capture every interaction within the system, how can institutions ensure that financial structures remain stable as they continue evolving?

That question leads to the next stage of the discussion.

Beyond psychology and modeling lies a deeper force shaping financial systems in ways that are often difficult to see.

That force is complexity itself.

Chapter 9

Complexity and Fragility

Financial systems rarely collapse because of a single event. In retrospect, crises are often described as though triggered by a single decisive moment: a market crash, a bank failure, a sovereign default, or the sudden collapse of a major institution. Yet these visible events are seldom the true beginning of instability; more often, they mark the point at which a system that has been under strain for some time finally reaches its limits.

Financial systems evolve continuously. Institutions adapt to new technologies, markets expand across borders, regulatory frameworks shift, and investors pursue new strategies for allocating capital. Each development introduces additional layers of connection within the financial system. Banks lend to one another. Asset managers trade securities issued by corporations operating in multiple countries. Derivatives link the performance of one asset to another across entirely different markets. Over time, these relationships accumulate, and the system becomes a network of institutions, markets, and instruments whose interactions extend far beyond the transactions that first created them.

For long periods, this interconnected structure can appear extraordinarily strong. Modern financial markets are remarkably efficient at moving capital across the global economy. Investors can allocate resources across continents within seconds. Pension funds in one country can finance infrastructure in another. Corporations raise capital from investors thousands of miles away. Technology enables financial institutions to process enormous volumes of transactions in real time, creating a level of speed and liquidity that previous generations could scarcely have imagined.

From the outside, such a system appears not only powerful but resilient.

Yet complexity carries a hidden cost.

As systems become more intricate, the relationships between their components grow harder to understand. A change in one part of the system may produce consequences elsewhere that are not immediately visible. The more connections exist, the more pathways there are through which disturbances can travel. Complex systems, therefore, possess a paradoxical quality. They can appear stable for long periods while quietly accumulating fragility beneath the surface.

This dynamic is not unique to finance. Similar patterns appear throughout the natural and engineered world. Large ecosystems, electrical grids, transportation networks, and global supply chains all reveal the same underlying principle. As systems expand and interconnect, they often become more efficient but can also become more sensitive to disruptions.

Efficiency and resilience are not always the same thing.

A system optimized for speed and productivity may have fewer buffers to absorb shocks when conditions change. In stable environments, that efficiency can produce remarkable performance. But when disturbances occur, tightly interconnected systems can rapidly transmit them across the network.

Finance is no exception.

Over the past several decades, financial markets have grown dramatically more complex. New instruments have been developed to manage risk, improve liquidity, and provide investors with increasingly specialized ways to allocate capital. Derivatives allow institutions to hedge exposures across currencies, interest rates, and commodities. Structured products transform pools of assets into tradable securities. Exchange-traded funds enable investors to gain exposure to entire markets through a single transaction. Algorithmic trading systems execute transactions at speeds measured in microseconds.

Each of these innovations serves a legitimate purpose. Individually, they can improve market functioning by increasing flexibility and expanding the range of tools available to investors. Financial innovation has enabled capital to flow more efficiently to businesses, governments, and projects that require funding.

Collectively, however, these innovations transform the structure of the financial system.

Layers of interdependence emerge between institutions, markets, and instruments. Banks lend to hedge funds that trade derivatives linked to corporate securities. Those corporations finance their operations through debt held by pension funds, whose assets are managed by investment firms that, in turn, rely on short-term funding from the banking system. The network becomes increasingly dense, and as that density grows, stress finds more paths through the system.

One reason complexity becomes so entrenched is that it often arrives disguised as sophistication. Financial innovation is rarely introduced as a source of fragility. It is presented as a solution. A product promises to improve liquidity. A structure promises to distribute risk more efficiently. A model promises greater precision in understanding exposure. Each new layer appears to make the system smarter, faster, and more adaptive.

This is what makes complexity so seductive.

Institutions are naturally drawn to tools that appear to improve performance while reducing uncertainty. Investors reward firms that deliver efficiency and innovation.

Regulators may initially welcome structures that seem to distribute risk more broadly across the system. Market participants, therefore, come to interpret greater complexity as evidence of advancement.

The system becomes more capable. Or so it appears.

Yet complexity often grows faster than understanding.

That imbalance is where fragility begins to emerge. When disturbances occur within relatively simple systems, their effects tend to remain localized. When disturbances occur within complex networks, however, they can travel rapidly across multiple channels, affecting participants who may have had little direct involvement in the original event.

Again, the global financial crisis of 2008 revealed this dynamic with unusual clarity. At its core, the crisis began with rising defaults in the United States housing market. Under ordinary circumstances, losses in one segment of the mortgage market might have remained relatively contained. Yet the structure of the financial system had evolved in ways that spread those risks across a vast network of institutions.

Mortgage loans were bundled into securities and sold to investors worldwide. Those securities were divided into tranches with different levels of risk and return. Financial institutions then created derivatives linked to those securities, allowing investors to gain exposure without directly owning the underlying loans. Risk had been distributed widely throughout the system.

For years, that distribution appeared to strengthen stability. If risks were spread across many institutions rather than concentrated in a few, the system should, in theory, have become more resilient.

In practice, however, the complexity of these structures made it extraordinarily difficult to determine where risk ultimately resided.

This is one of the most dangerous features of financial complexity. Risk can be moved without being reduced.

It can be repackaged, subdivided, referenced, hedged, and sold, creating the appearance that exposure has been dispersed when in fact it may simply have become harder to trace. A mortgage may begin as a loan issued by a local lender. It may then be pooled with thousands of other loans, converted into a security, divided into tranches, sold to multiple institutions, and referenced by derivatives held by entirely different counterparties. At each stage, the connection between the original risk and its ultimate holders becomes more difficult to map.

By the time stress emerges, few participants understand the full chain.

When housing prices began declining, and mortgage defaults increased, uncertainty spread rapidly. Institutions were unsure which counterparties held the greatest exposures or how losses might cascade through interconnected contracts. Trust began to erode.

Financial markets depend fundamentally on confidence. Institutions lend to one another because they believe their counterparties are solvent. When that confidence weakens, participants become reluctant to extend credit. During the crisis, uncertainty about exposures embedded in complex financial structures led institutions to withdraw liquidity from one another. The result was a sudden tightening of credit conditions across global markets.

This episode revealed a central vulnerability of complex systems: opacity.

As financial structures become more elaborate, it becomes increasingly difficult for participants, including highly sophisticated institutions, to understand the full extent of their exposures. Information may be dispersed across multiple organizations, jurisdictions, and instruments. Without transparency, complexity can mask fragility.

Opacity does more than conceal risk. It also delays response.

Participants in transparent systems can respond earlier when warning signs emerge because underlying exposures are visible enough to evaluate. In opaque systems, however, institutions often continue operating under assumptions of stability because they cannot clearly see where vulnerabilities are accumulating. This delay can prove devastating. By the time markets recognize that confidence has been misplaced, institutions may simultaneously attempt to reduce exposure. Assets are sold into declining markets. Liquidity disappears. Prices fall rapidly, not only because fundamentals have worsened, but because participants no longer trust the structure itself.

Complexity, therefore, influences behavior as much as it influences risk.

This does not mean complexity should be eliminated. Financial innovation often produces genuine benefits, enabling more efficient capital allocation and more sophisticated tools for managing exposure. The challenge lies in balancing innovation with clarity. When financial systems grow faster than the ability to understand them, stability becomes harder to maintain.

That task is difficult because complexity evolves organically. No single institution designs the financial system as a whole. Markets grow through countless independent decisions made by banks, asset managers, corporations, regulators, and investors. Each participant acts within a particular set of incentives and constraints. Yet the cumulative effect of those decisions shapes the system's architecture. Over time, that architecture may develop characteristics that no individual participant fully anticipated.

Leverage provides a clear example of how these dynamics interact. Leverage allows investors to amplify returns by borrowing capital to expand positions. Used responsibly, it can support economic growth by enabling institutions to finance productive investment. But leverage also increases sensitivity to price movements. Within complex systems, leverage can create feedback loops that magnify instability. When asset prices fall, investors using leverage may be forced to sell holdings to meet margin calls or reduce debt. Those sales push prices lower, triggering additional margin calls and further selling.

The process becomes self-reinforcing.

What begins as a moderate decline can escalate into a sharp contraction as institutions respond simultaneously to similar pressures. These dynamics illustrate a broader principle of complex financial systems. Fragility often arises not from a single irrational decision, but from the interaction of many seemingly rational ones.

Institutions acting prudently within their own frameworks may still contribute to systemic risk when their actions intersect within an interconnected network. A strategy that appears sound in isolation may produce unintended consequences when adopted widely across the market.

Understanding this requires a shift in perspective. Risk cannot be evaluated solely at the level of the individual institution or the individual investment. It must also be considered at the relationship level. Systemic risk emerges from the connections between institutions, markets, and instruments. Those relationships determine how disturbances travel and whether they dissipate or intensify.

For those responsible for allocating capital, this insight carries important implications. Effective stewardship requires more than analyzing individual assets. It requires awareness of the larger system in which those assets exist. Investors must consider not only the characteristics of specific investments, but also how those investments interact with the broader financial environment. They must ask where leverage concentrations are building, how liquidity may behave under stress, which institutional relationships could amplify disturbances, and whether the structures generating attractive returns are transparent enough to justify trust.

These questions rarely yield simple answers. But they encourage a more complete understanding of risk.

Complex systems demand humility from those who operate within them. Even experienced participants must acknowledge that their view of the whole will always remain partial. Yet that recognition can lead to wiser decisions. Institutions that understand the fragility inherent in complex systems are more likely to adopt structures oriented toward resilience rather than short-term optimization. They emphasize transparency, diversification, and prudent risk management rather than relying solely on models that assume stability will continue indefinitely.

In doing so, they strengthen the broader financial architecture.

Because stability within complex systems does not emerge automatically, it must be cultivated through thoughtful design, responsible stewardship, and an awareness of how individual decisions shape the collective environment.

Even within complex systems, however, capital continues to move. Investment decisions are made every day by individuals and institutions seeking returns, managing risk, or pursuing broader objectives. Those decisions determine not only the distribution of financial resources, but also the direction of economic development.

Which raises the next fundamental question.

If the movement of capital shapes the structure of economies and societies, who ultimately determines where that capital flows?

Behind every allocation decision lies a force rarely discussed openly, yet quietly influencing markets around the world.

Power.

Chapter 10

The Concentration of Capital Power

Capital does not move randomly. Every day, trillions of dollars flow through financial markets as investors purchase securities, institutions rebalance portfolios, corporations raise financing, and governments deploy resources to influence economic outcomes. On the surface, these movements appear to reflect countless independent decisions made by participants across the global financial system. Markets process information continuously, responding to new data, changing expectations, and shifting perceptions of risk. From a distance, it can seem as though capital flows through the system, naturally moving toward the opportunities that offer the most attractive returns.

Yet beneath this appearance of decentralization lies a powerful organizing force. The direction of capital is shaped, to a remarkable degree, by the decisions of a relatively small number of actors whose influence extends across industries, geographies, and generations. Large institutional investors, pension funds, sovereign wealth funds, insurance companies, endowments, foundations, and global asset managers control enormous pools of capital. Their allocation decisions help determine which industries expand, which technologies receive funding, which real estate markets strengthen, which infrastructure is built, and which regions attract long-term economic development.

This is one of the defining realities of modern finance. The financial system comprises millions of participants, but much of its power flows through a far smaller number of institutions. The scale at which those institutions operate gives their decisions consequences that extend far beyond any individual transaction. When they adjust portfolios, rebalance exposures, or shift strategic priorities, entire sectors of the economy can feel the effect.

The scale involved is difficult to overstate. A major pension fund increasing its allocation to infrastructure can mobilize billions of dollars toward transportation networks, utilities, data centers, water systems, and energy projects. A sovereign wealth fund investing in emerging technologies can accelerate the growth of industries ranging from artificial intelligence to biotechnology. A large asset manager changing its exposure to a sector can alter demand for securities across the market, affecting valuations, liquidity, and the cost of capital for firms operating within that space.

Because of this scale, institutional conviction carries weight.

Financial markets are often described as neutral systems that reflect the collective judgment of millions of investors. Prices rise or fall as supply and demand respond to new information, and capital flows toward opportunities offering attractive risk-adjusted returns. This description captures an important part of how markets function. But it does not fully capture how influence operates within modern finance.

Institutional investors do not simply participate in markets. At a sufficient scale, they help shape them.

Sovereign wealth funds offer one of the clearest examples. These funds manage national savings generated from natural resources, trade surpluses, or long-term fiscal reserves. Some command pools of capital exceeding one trillion dollars. When institutions of this size deploy capital, they do not merely seek returns in a narrow sense. Their decisions can influence real estate markets, infrastructure projects, private company financing, and the strategic direction of multinational corporations.

Pension funds exercise a similar kind of influence, though in a different form. They manage the retirement savings of millions of workers and must allocate capital in ways that preserve purchasing power and meet obligations extending far into the future. Their investment strategies, therefore, tend to emphasize diversification, durability, and long-horizon stability. Yet the cumulative effect of those decisions extends far beyond the beneficiaries whose savings they steward.

When pension funds collectively favor particular asset classes, whether public equities, private equity, real estate, infrastructure, private credit, or alternative strategies, they influence valuations across those markets. Their allocations attract additional investors, increase liquidity within favored sectors, and shape the availability of financing for businesses seeking capital.

Asset managers play an equally significant role. Over the past several decades, the global asset management industry has grown dramatically. Large firms now oversee trillions of dollars on behalf of clients ranging from individuals and families to governments and charitable institutions. Through portfolio construction, model design, security selection, and asset allocation frameworks, these firms help determine how capital is distributed across the global economy.

The result is a financial system increasingly shaped by the concentration of capital within a relatively small number of institutions.

This concentration does not require explicit coordination to exert influence. It emerges through the collective behavior of institutions operating within similar frameworks, responding to similar incentives, and often reaching similar conclusions about where capital should go. That distinction matters. The power of concentrated capital in modern finance does not usually resemble a conspiracy. It is structural rather than theatrical. Institutions do not need to gather in a room to decide the future of a sector; they can shape it by acting. They need only operate at a sufficient scale within similar assumptions. When many large allocators evaluate the world through similar lenses, capital flows can become highly concentrated without any formal collaboration.

One of the clearest examples of this dynamic is the rise of passive investing. Over the past several decades, index funds and exchange-traded funds have grown dramatically. These vehicles direct enormous volumes of capital into benchmarks that allocate weight according to market capitalization. As investors increasingly allocate assets to these strategies, capital automatically flows toward the companies already holding the largest positions in the index.

This process is not ideological. It is mechanical.

Funds track the same benchmark, purchasing similar securities in proportion to their index weights. As assets under management rise, the flow of capital into those securities expands accordingly. Over time, the index's structure begins to influence where new capital enters the market.

This illustrates an important feature of modern financial systems. Capital often moves according to rules embedded within investment frameworks. Those rules shape outcomes. They influence which firms enjoy lower capital costs, which sectors attract sustained investor attention, and which regions gain easier access to financing. What appears to be a neutral process of participation can therefore reinforce existing concentrations of economic influence.

This matters because the institutions directing capital do not merely react to markets. In many cases, they help create them. Their decisions affect demand for securities, industry valuations, credit availability, and the pace at which emerging sectors receive support. When capital is concentrated in relatively few hands, the priorities of those institutions begin to shape the broader financial landscape.

That influence extends well beyond public equity markets. Private markets, including venture capital, private equity, infrastructure, and private credit, also reflect the force of large allocators. Pension funds, endowments, sovereign wealth funds, and family offices frequently provide the capital that enables these vehicles. Their commitments determine how much funding flows into emerging companies, industrial transformation, logistics networks, and complex lending structures.

In many cases, the most consequential economic decisions occur long before they become visible to the public. A venture investment made at the earliest stage may determine whether a company ever reaches scale; a private infrastructure commitment may shape whether a region gains the capacity to endure. A private credit allocation may provide financing to businesses that conventional banks no longer serve. A real estate mandate may alter the development pattern of entire communities.

In each case, capital is doing more than seeking financial return. It is shaping the architecture of possibility. That phrase matters because it reveals what is so often concealed by the language of finance. Capital is frequently discussed in terms of portfolios, mandates, benchmarks, and expected returns. Those categories are necessary, but they can obscure what capital is actually doing in the world. Capital builds, extends, withholds, accelerates, and delays. It determines what receives the time and resources required to become real.

For this reason, allocation at scale is never merely financial.

It is civilizational.

The infrastructure that supports modern societies, transportation systems, power grids, housing, hospitals, communication networks, manufacturing corridors, research campuses, and data infrastructure often depends on investment capital. The direction of capital, therefore, affects not only corporate balance sheets but the lived structure of economic life itself.

Hospitals expand when projects receive financing. Energy systems evolve when investors support new infrastructure. Supply chains become more resilient when capital funds domestic capacity or strategic redundancy. Community strengthens when capital supports durable institutions rather than transient extraction.

Where capital goes, development follows. Where capital hesitates, growth slows. Where capital withdraws, decline often begins.

For this reason, the power of capital is often underestimated precisely because it operates so quietly. It rarely appears in dramatic public form. It is embedded in committee decisions, portfolio mandates, investment memoranda, due diligence processes, and model allocations. Its influence is expressed through percentages and approvals rather than through speeches and headlines.

Yet its consequences are tangible.

Communities with sustained access to investment often gain jobs, infrastructure, and institutional capacity. Communities bypassed by capital may experience declining business formation, deteriorating services, and fewer pathways toward resilience. Entire sectors can rise because capital made them viable, while others can languish because financing never reached them in time or at a sufficient scale.

Recognizing this connection does not require abandoning financial discipline. On the contrary, discipline becomes even more important once one understands the weight capital carries. The point is not that every allocator must become a social planner. It is that the discipline of finance alone does not erase the wider consequences of capital allocation. A portfolio decision may be analytically sound within its own framework and still produce broader structural effects beyond what that framework captures. Large allocators, especially, cannot avoid shaping the world simply by insisting that they are only following the numbers.

The numbers themselves do not direct the world. People do.

This is where the question of stewardship becomes more urgent.

Those who allocate capital are not merely participants in markets. They are stewards of resources that shape economic development, technological direction, institutional durability, and social possibility. Yet the connection between capital allocation and societal consequence is not always fully recognized within financial decision-making frameworks.

Most institutions focus primarily on risk-adjusted return, seeking to optimize performance within established mandates. This objective is essential for fulfilling fiduciary duties to clients and beneficiaries. However, it can also narrow the field of vision. When performance becomes the only language through which decisions are evaluated, the wider consequences of allocation can disappear beneath the surface of financial discipline. This narrowing is understandable. Institutions are hired to perform, and performance is often measured over compressed time horizons. Portfolio managers are evaluated relative to benchmarks. Capital is allocated based on recent results. Risk is defined not only by absolute loss, but by deviation from peers.

Within this structure, decisions that align with prevailing market behavior often appear prudent, even when they reinforce systemic vulnerabilities. As Kate Raworth has observed, "Today's financial system is designed to deliver short-term returns, not long-term value."

This design does not arise from any single decision. It emerges gradually, shaped by incentives, measurement frameworks, and institutional expectations. Over time, these forces concentrate attention on what can be measured quickly and rewarded immediately, while outcomes that require patience, resilience, or long-term commitment receive less emphasis. What appears efficient at the institutional level may, at the system level, produce fragility.

Scale changes the nature of responsibility.

A small investor allocating capital within a personal account does not carry the same systemic influence as a sovereign wealth fund, a global asset manager, or a pension system representing millions of workers. As the scale of capital increases, so too does the breadth of its consequences.

At a sufficient scale, capital allocation begins to resemble governance. Not governance in the political sense, but in the economic sense. Decisions about which sectors receive financing, which projects are funded, which firms gain durability, and which technologies are brought to scale ultimately shape the structure of economies and the opportunities available within them.

In recent years, frameworks such as environmental, social, and governance (ESG) have emerged as a response to this expanding field of consequence. These frameworks aim to evaluate capital deployment beyond traditional financial metrics, providing greater visibility into how investment decisions influence environmental systems, social outcomes, and institutional behavior. Their rise reflects a broader recognition that capital does not operate in isolation, but within interconnected systems whose stability and direction are shaped by financial flows.

Yet ESG remains, by design, a framework that is structured, measurable, and often applied through standardized criteria. Stewardship operates at a different level. It is not defined by metrics alone, but by judgment, responsibility, and a sustained awareness of consequence over time. ESG can inform how capital is evaluated, but stewardship defines the obligation to allocate it with discipline in the first place. Frameworks can guide decisions, but they cannot substitute for the responsibility required to make them.

This is one of the central realities of modern finance.

Power now operates through allocation.

Governments remain important, of course. Regulation, taxation, and public policy continue to shape markets profoundly. But alongside formal political authority, another kind of influence exists. It is quieter, less theatrical, and often more difficult to observe directly. It is the influence exercised by those who decide where large pools of capital will go.

This reality raises questions that cannot be answered solely through portfolio mathematics. What principles guide those who hold this power? What disciplines restrain the temptation to treat capital purely as influence without responsibility? How should institutions think about fiduciary duty when the scale of their capital shapes not only returns, but the structure of economic life itself?

These are not simple questions, and the modern financial world has not produced a single settled answer. Some argue that financial institutions should focus exclusively on return, leaving social priorities to governments and civil society. Others contend that institutions controlling vast pools of capital cannot ignore the broader consequences of their decisions.

This debate has appeared in many forms. It can be seen in discussions surrounding environmental, social, and governance frameworks. It appears in discussions about impact investing, public-market stewardship, sustainable infrastructure, and long-horizon capital allocation. It appears whenever institutions ask whether capital should merely respond to the world as it is or help shape the world that is coming.

Whatever position one takes within these debates, one fact remains clear.

Capital allocation is a form of power.

And power without discipline always invites distortion.

This is why the concentration of capital power cannot be treated as a neutral development. It is neither inherently virtuous nor inherently destructive. Its consequences depend on the character, discipline, and governing philosophy of those who hold it. Capital can support innovation, infrastructure, and durable prosperity when allocated responsibly. It can also intensify instability, inequality, and short-horizon extraction when deployed without sufficient awareness of its broader effects.

The concentration of power, therefore, does not eliminate the need for stewardship.

It makes stewardship indispensable.

This is where the book begins to turn more fully from diagnosis toward responsibility. The question is no longer how capital behaves inside systems, or how complexity and incentives distort its movement. The question becomes: who is responsible for directing that force, and according to what standard?

Because once capital reaches sufficient scale, the issue is no longer return. It is judgment, restraint, and moral seriousness in the presence of enormous financial consequences.

The modern financial system has no shortage of intelligence. It has no shortage of data, models, strategies, or innovation. What it too often lacks is a language equal to the responsibility embedded in the act of allocation.

This is the deeper implication of concentrated capital power. The larger the pool of capital, the more consequential the discipline governing its direction must become. It is here that stewardship moves from aspiration to necessity.

Because the question is no longer whether capital shapes the world.

It does.

The true question is whether those who direct it are prepared to carry its weight.

What emerges from these systems is not abstract. It is structural. Capital does not simply respond to markets. At scale, this influence becomes decisive, shaping which institutions survive, which industries are elevated, and which possibilities become real.

Over time, these decisions accumulate. What appears as participation becomes influence. What appears as allocation becomes direction. The architecture of economies is not formed all at once, but through the repeated movement of capital within systems that reinforce certain outcomes while constraining others.

At this point, the language of neutrality begins to break down. Capital is often described as a tool, something that can be directed without consequence beyond the immediate transaction. But capital does not operate outside the systems it influences. It participates in their construction, shaping conditions that extend far beyond any single decision.

What matters, then, is how capital is carried. Because once capital reaches sufficient scale, allocation becomes responsibility.

What follows is stewardship.

Part III

Stewardship and Responsibility

"The ultimate test of a system is not how it performs,
but how it endures over time."

Heather Desjardins

Chapter 11

Stewarding the Weight of Capital

Stewardship begins with recognition. Capital does not become consequential only at scale. It is consequential from the moment it is directed. What changes at scale is not its nature, but the magnitude of its effect. To allocate capital is to influence outcomes over time. Those outcomes extend beyond individual transactions, shaping which systems strengthen, which institutions endure, and which possibilities are allowed to develop.

Stewardship is not a matter of intention. It is a matter of discipline. It requires the ability to evaluate not only immediate outcomes but also the longer-term effects of allocating across systems that evolve over time. Decisions must be made with an awareness of how capital reinforces certain structures, directs resources toward particular uses, and influences the conditions under which future choices are made. Without this discipline, capital amplifies existing patterns, often in ways that are not immediately visible.

When stewardship is absent, the effects are not immediate. Systems rarely fail all at once. Instead, small distortions accumulate as capital continues to be directed without full recognition of its broader impact. Incentives begin to diverge from long-term outcomes, and decisions that appear rational in isolation contribute to imbalances at scale. Over time, these imbalances shape market conditions, concentrating risk, narrowing access, and reinforcing dynamics that become increasingly difficult to reverse.

Disciplined stewardship requires more than technical proficiency. It requires the ability to evaluate how individual decisions interact with the systems in which they occur. Allocation must be approached with an understanding of second-order effects, where outcomes extend beyond the immediate transaction and influence broader patterns over time.

This includes recognizing how capital reinforces incentives, shapes access, and contributes to structures that may persist long after the initial decision has been made.

What distinguishes a steward from a participant is not access to capital, but the standard applied to its use. A participant responds to incentives as they appear, optimizing within the system's constraints. A steward recognizes those same incentives but evaluates them within a broader frame, considering how each decision contributes to outcomes that extend beyond the immediate context. This distinction is not always visible in the moment, but it becomes clear over time as the effects of allocation accumulate.

At scale, this distinction becomes more consequential. Large pools of capital, including pension systems, endowments, and sovereign funds, do not simply participate in markets. Their allocation decisions influence how those markets function. When capital is directed with a narrow focus on short-term performance, incentives can become misaligned with long-term stability. When guided with discipline and an awareness of broader impact, it can support structures that are more durable over time. In this way, stewardship is not an abstract ideal. It is reflected in the patterns that capital creates across systems.

It is within this broader context that the concept of risk must be understood.

Risk occupies a central place in financial decision-making, yet it is most often defined within a narrow analytical frame. In modern finance, risk is typically understood as the probability of loss, the volatility of returns, or the potential deviation from expected outcomes. These measures provide an essential structure for evaluating investments, comparing opportunities, and maintaining discipline across portfolios. They allow institutions to operate at scale, translating uncertainty into a form that can be monitored, governed, and acted upon with consistency.

This framework is necessary, but it is not complete.

By focusing primarily on how assets behave within portfolios, conventional definitions of risk capture the immediate exposure associated with a given allocation. They evaluate how positions may respond to changes in market conditions, how correlations may shift, and how losses may emerge under stress. What they do not fully capture is how the repeated direction of capital influences the environment in which those assets exist. Over time, patterns of allocation do more than express views on risk and return. They reinforce certain structures, reward particular behaviors, and shape the environment in which markets function. As capital flows toward specific strategies, sectors, or financial structures, it contributes to their expansion. As participation increases, these structures gain depth, liquidity, and apparent stability. Market confidence strengthens, and assumptions that once required scrutiny begin to feel validated through repetition. In this way, allocation does not simply respond to existing conditions. It participates in their construction.

The consequences of this process are rarely visible in isolation. Individual decisions appear rational within their immediate context, supported by data, models, and prevailing market signals. Yet when similar decisions are made across institutions, guided by comparable incentives and analytical frameworks, their cumulative effect becomes more significant. What appears as independent judgment at the portfolio level can produce convergence at the system level, reinforcing the same assumptions across increasingly large pools of capital.

It is within this convergence that a more structural form of risk begins to emerge.

This form of risk differs from traditional measures. It does not manifest as short-term volatility or immediate loss. Instead, it develops through the gradual alignment of behavior, the reinforcement of shared assumptions, and the increasing dependence of markets on conditions that may not persist. Stability in such environments depends on continued participation rather than on underlying resilience.

Financial history offers repeated examples of this dynamic. Periods of sustained growth often coincide with rising confidence in prevailing strategies, greater leverage, and the widespread adoption of similar risk-evaluation models. During these periods, measured risk may appear contained even as underlying vulnerability expands. The absence of visible stress reinforces the belief that existing frameworks are sufficient, allowing exposure to build in ways that are not immediately apparent.

When conditions change, the adjustment is rarely confined to individual positions. Because the system has adapted around shared assumptions, responses tend to occur simultaneously. Efforts to reduce exposure, preserve liquidity, or manage loss can amplify the very instability they are intended to contain. What was previously experienced as stability reveals itself as fragility, shaped not by a single decision but by the accumulated direction of capital over time.

Recognizing this distinction does not diminish the value of traditional risk management. Quantitative models, stress testing, and disciplined portfolio construction remain essential tools for navigating uncertainty. They provide clarity within complexity and allow institutions to operate with a degree of control that would otherwise be impossible. The limitation lies not in their use but in the assumption that they capture the full scope of risk embedded in financial systems.

The responsibility of those who allocate capital, therefore, extends beyond the management of portfolio-level exposure. It requires awareness of how allocation decisions interact across the system, shaping conditions that influence future outcomes. This awareness cannot be derived solely from data. It depends on judgment, experience, and a willingness to examine not only whether an investment is attractive under current conditions, but also whether those conditions are becoming less stable as a result of repeated participation.

For institutions operating at scale, this challenge becomes more pronounced. Large pools of capital do not merely participate in markets; they influence them. Their allocations affect pricing, liquidity, and the relative attractiveness of entire sectors. As others respond to these signals, patterns of behavior can become self-reinforcing, extending the reach of initial decisions far beyond their original context.

In this environment, the question is not whether risk can be eliminated. It cannot. Risk remains inseparable from investment, innovation, and economic growth. The more relevant question is how risk is understood, and whether the frameworks used to evaluate it are sufficient for the scale and complexity of modern financial systems.

Stewardship introduces a broader discipline into this process. It asks those entrusted with capital to consider not only the immediate characteristics of an investment, but also the conditions it supports and the structures it reinforces over time. It requires attention to the relationship between individual decisions and system-wide outcomes, recognizing that the cumulative effect of allocation can either strengthen resilience or contribute to instability.

This perspective does not replace existing risk frameworks. It extends them, integrating technical analysis with a deeper awareness of consequence. It acknowledges that capital allocation is not only a response to markets but also a force that shapes them, and that the risks most likely to define future outcomes may emerge gradually through the interaction of incentives, behavior, and scale.

For this reason, the discipline of stewardship becomes essential. It provides a framework for carrying uncertainty without reducing it to abstraction, and for directing capital with an awareness of the structures that decisions help create.

Because the deepest challenge of capital is not simply that it involves risk, but that its influence extends beyond what conventional definitions of risk are designed to measure. Stewardship provides the discipline required to recognize that influence and to direct it with awareness of the structures it helps create.

This is where stewardship defines the outcome.

Chapter 12

The Character Required of the Steward

Power without responsibility eventually erodes the systems that sustain it.

This principle applies as much to financial systems as it does to political, civic, or social institutions. Whenever capital becomes concentrated in the hands of those responsible for allocating it, the decisions surrounding that capital inevitably carry consequences that extend far beyond individual transactions. The larger the scale of the capital, the wider the field of consequence. At that level, the central question is no longer simply whether the allocator is skilled. The deeper question is whether the allocator possesses the character required to carry that responsibility well.

Modern financial discourse rarely speaks in these terms.

Performance metrics, portfolio returns, volatility measures, benchmark comparisons, fee structures, and quarterly reporting cycles dominate the language of markets. These tools are essential, and no serious steward of capital can ignore them. Yet they capture only part of the influence embedded in capital allocation. They describe how an investment performs. They do not necessarily reveal what patterns of allocation are gradually building, strengthening, weakening, or leaving behind.

These limitations become clearer when examining how capital is actually allocated in practice. Portfolio managers operate within investment committees. Analysts evaluate companies through financial statements, cost structures, revenue projections, and valuation models. Asset allocators build portfolios according to expectations about diversification, correlation, and risk exposure across asset classes. Credit committees evaluate collateral, terms, and repayment capacity. Institutional leaders review recommendations through the discipline of fiduciary duty and organizational mandate.

Each decision is framed within professional structures designed to optimize financial outcomes.

Within that structure, it can become easy to forget the scale of influence those decisions carry. An allocation committee may review a proposal primarily through projected returns and risk exposures. Analysts may debate assumptions about growth, margins, or interest rate sensitivity. Portfolio managers may shift capital by only a few percentage points to maintain portfolio balance or respond to changing market conditions.

Individually, these actions appear routine.

Yet when multiplied across institutions controlling billions or trillions of dollars, these same decisions help determine the direction of entire industries. A modest increase in institutional investment toward renewable energy can accelerate infrastructure development across continents. A reduction in lending to certain sectors can reshape employment patterns across communities. Sustained capital flows toward emerging technologies can alter the trajectory of innovation for decades.

Capital moves quietly, but its consequences are rarely small.

For this reason, the question of stewardship cannot be answered solely through process. Governance matters. Prudence matters. Analytical rigor matters. But ultimately, capital is directed through human judgment, and human judgment is inseparable from character.

This is where the idea of the steward becomes more than a metaphor. Stewardship is an ancient concept because it describes enduring responsibility. Across cultures and traditions, the steward was the individual entrusted with the care of resources that affected others' lives. The steward did not simply possess what had been placed under their care. They were expected to preserve it, direct it wisely, and manage it in ways that honored both present need and future consequence.

Historically, the steward might have been responsible for land, estates, household supplies, or communal assets. The principle remained the same. Stewardship requires more than maintaining value in a narrow sense. It required managing resources in ways that sustained the people and institutions that depended on them.

The steward therefore served both the present and the future.

In modern finance, this responsibility appears most clearly in the concept of fiduciary duty. Pension trustees safeguard retirement savings that may not be accessed for decades. Investment managers are entrusted with capital representing years of labor and deferred consumption. Insurance institutions maintain reserves to cover obligations that may arise far into the future. Endowments and foundations must preserve resources not only for current operations but for the continuation of their mission across generations.

These responsibilities are not merely technical requirements.

They reflect a deeper trust placed in financial institutions by the individuals and communities whose resources they oversee. Workers contribute portions of their income to pension systems, expecting those funds to be managed prudently. Families entrust their savings to professionals whose decisions may shape whether those resources grow with enough resilience to support future needs. Governments establish sovereign wealth funds to preserve national assets for generations yet to be born. Universities, hospitals, and charitable institutions rely on investment decisions that determine whether their missions can endure.

In every case, capital represents accumulated human effort.

It reflects work, discipline, restraint, sacrifice, enterprise, and hope. It embodies the labor of the past and the expectations of the future. Once this reality becomes clear, the meaning of financial responsibility expands. Allocation is no longer simply the movement of capital across balance sheet categories. It becomes the direction of human effort through time.

This is why character matters. A person may possess analytical brilliance without possessing steadiness. A person may be intelligent without being trustworthy. A person may understand markets without understanding consequences. Technical skill allows an individual to navigate complexity, but it cannot ensure that power will be carried with discipline, restraint, or integrity.

Intelligence and technical skill are not all that is needed. The steward must also be guided by truth, courage, and accountability.

Truthfulness in this context is more than honesty in the ordinary sense. It includes the willingness to see conditions as they are rather than as they would appear to optimism or fear. It means resisting the temptation to rationalize fragile assumptions simply because they are profitable in the moment. It requires acknowledging uncertainty where it exists, rather than disguising it beneath confidence or procedure.

Truth in Word and Practice begins here.

The steward must be able to see capital clearly. Every allocation strengthens, accelerates, reinforces, or withdraws from something. Capital never arrives without consequence. It shapes systems gradually through repeated direction over time.

For this reason, the steward must be able to speak honestly about valuation, leverage, fragility, concentration, and risk, even when those truths are uncomfortable. In financial systems, false clarity can be more dangerous than acknowledged uncertainty. The person entrusted with capital must therefore resist illusion, especially the illusion that recent success guarantees future safety.

This requires humility.

Humility is not weakness. In finance, it is often a source of strength. A disciplined allocator understands that models are limited, liquidity can disappear, and periods of stability often conceal vulnerabilities that only become visible under stress. Humility keeps judgment tethered to reality rather than momentum, reputation, or recent performance.

It also resists abstraction.

The steward understands that capital is never purely numerical. Behind every allocation sits accumulated human effort expressed through savings, labor, enterprise, retirement reserves, institutional capital, and long-term trust. Stewardship, therefore, requires more than technical competence. It requires the willingness to recognize what capital is reinforcing as it begins to move through systems.

Truth in Word and Practice rejects the idea that financial decisions exist in isolation from consequence. Capital shapes incentives, institutions, and future conditions, whether those effects are immediately visible or not.

Stewardship begins by seeing capital clearly.

Once a person begins to see what capital is reinforcing, the question becomes whether they will act with intention or drift with convenience. Financial systems reward speed, momentum, and participation. Courage introduces discipline to that drift.

The steward must therefore possess a quieter form of strength.

Courage in finance is rarely theatrical. It is not reckless contrarianism or permanent defensiveness. It is the discipline required to remain grounded when incentives reward excess, when optimism becomes fashionable, and when caution appears costly in the short term.

Financial history repeatedly demonstrates how powerful the pressure to conform can become. During rising markets, restraint can feel like failure. During speculative periods, prudence can appear unsophisticated. During moments of widespread enthusiasm, the willingness to ask difficult questions can isolate those who do.

The steward must be able to withstand that pressure.

This form of courage is inseparable from discipline and patience. The steward understands that not every opportunity deserves capital and not every trend deserves trust. The ability to wait, decline, reduce exposure, or step back when others accelerate is often one of the most difficult forms of discipline in finance.

The cost of caution is usually visible immediately.

The reward for caution often becomes visible only later, when systems are tested.

That difference in timing matters.

Short-term underperformance is highly visible. Long-term resilience often remains invisible until conditions deteriorate. For this reason, courage in stewardship requires the ability to act in accordance with standards deeper than immediate approval, market enthusiasm, or short-term validation.

The steward understands that discipline is not the absence of conviction. It is the ability to hold conviction without surrendering judgment to momentum, pressure, or the emotional atmosphere of the market.

Accountability as the Witness anchors stewardship over time.

Stewardship is revealed in patterns, not isolated decisions. It is revealed through the repeated direction of capital, the habits those allocations reinforce, and the long-term consequences that gradually emerge from them.

Modern financial systems often diffuse responsibility across layers of process, specialization, and institutional structure. One team originates the transaction. Another structures the vehicle. Another approves the allocation. Another manages the exposure. Another reports performance. In such environments, participants may remain accountable to procedure while no one remains fully accountable to consequence.

The steward resists that fragmentation.

Responsibility does not end where formal role descriptions do. Capital continues moving long after the original decision is made, shaping systems, incentives, institutions, and behaviors along the way. Accountability, therefore, requires understanding not only where capital is placed, but what that capital reinforces over time.

The steward asks different questions.

What habits does this allocation reward?

What dependencies does it create?

What forms of fragility, resilience, concentration, or stability may emerge from its repeated direction?

These effects are rarely visible immediately. They accumulate gradually through systems that respond to the incentives capital strengthens over time.

Accountability begins when excuses end.

It requires the willingness to say not only "I followed procedure," but also "I am responsible for what this decision helped create."

Trust emerges from this seriousness of responsibility.

Financial systems depend on trust in ways that are often underestimated. Contracts may be written, trades cleared, and assets held by custodians in accordance with detailed rules. Yet beneath these mechanisms lies a shared belief that institutions act with sufficient integrity and seriousness to preserve the system itself. When trust weakens, capital becomes more defensive, more expensive, and more fragile. Liquidity withdraws, cooperation narrows, and hidden vulnerabilities begin to surface.

Trust, therefore, functions as an invisible foundation beneath financial systems.

And trust is sustained not by intelligence alone, but by character.

The steward must also cultivate a disciplined relationship with time.

Investment decisions are often evaluated through quarterly or annual reporting cycles. These measures are necessary, but they are not sufficient for responsibility. Some of the most consequential capital decisions unfold across decades. Infrastructure, health systems, manufacturing capacity, environmental resilience, and foundational research often require patient capital that cannot be fully justified within short reporting periods.

The steward must be capable of seeing beyond those cycles without dismissing them.

Stewardship requires holding present obligations and future consequences together. It demands seriousness about time itself. The steward asks not only whether a decision serves the next quarter or the next year, but whether it strengthens or weakens the conditions future generations will inherit.

For this reason, institutions with long horizons carry particular importance.

Pension funds, endowments, sovereign funds, and intergenerational family offices are uniquely positioned to practice stewardship because the capital they oversee is intended to endure. Yet, duration alone is not enough. A long-term horizon without disciplined character can lead to poor judgment. True stewardship requires the pairing of time and principle.

The steward must hold complexity without surrendering clarity.

Modern finance is complex: derivative instruments, layered financing structures, global counterparties, and interconnected markets. No individual can master every variable. Yet the steward can maintain a posture of clarity by refusing to surrender judgment entirely to complexity.

This means asking whether a structure is understandable enough to deserve trust. It means recognizing when sophistication becomes opacity. It means resisting the temptation to accept confidence in place of comprehension.

Such clarity requires inner steadiness.

It also requires freedom from vanity.

Vanity can appear in many forms within finance: the desire to appear certain, the hunger to outperform at any cost, the reluctance to admit uncertainty, or the need to maintain prestige in front of peers and clients. When these impulses govern decision-making, capital becomes a stage for ambition rather than a responsibility carried with care.

For this reason, stewardship is not merely a professional function. It is a discipline of character.

Character determines how power is exercised when external constraints are weak. It determines whether truth is spoken when optimism would be easier, whether restraint is practiced when expansion appears profitable, and whether decisions remain anchored to consequence rather than prestige or habit.

These qualities become most important during periods of market enthusiasm.

When asset prices rise rapidly and strategies appear consistently profitable, institutions may feel pressure to increase exposure to remain competitive. Boards reward visible growth. Clients demand higher returns. Organizations fear appearing cautious, while others accelerate.

In such environments, discipline becomes rare.

And it is precisely during those moments that character matters most.

Because what protects financial systems from excess is rarely brilliance alone. More often, it is restraint, honesty, and the willingness to remain grounded when the atmosphere encourages inflation of both exposure and confidence.

The same is true during a crisis.

Moments of instability test not only portfolios and institutions but also the people responsible for them. When uncertainty spreads and confidence contracts, the steward is revealed by response. Does leadership retreat into self-protection alone, or remain capable of stabilizing action where possible? Does communication remain clear, or dissolve into abstraction? Does the institution honor the seriousness of what others have entrusted to it?

These questions are ultimately questions of character.

And because financial institutions are interconnected, the answers matter beyond any single organization. The steadiness of one participant can stabilize a network. The panic of another can amplify fragility. In moments of stress, response becomes part of the system itself.

This leads to a deeper conclusion.

Stewardship is not merely about what one does with capital. It is about who one must become to carry capital well. The responsibility cannot be fulfilled through procedure alone. It requires habits of judgment, restraint, and truthfulness that shape conduct over time.

The future of capital, therefore, cannot be separated from the formation of those who direct it.

A financial system may possess extraordinary tools, global reach, and advanced analytics, yet remain vulnerable if the people entrusted with its power lack the discipline required to wield it responsibly. By contrast, even within imperfect systems, serious stewards can strengthen institutional integrity, preserve trust, and direct capital in ways that support durable prosperity.

Capital carries weight not only because of its scale, but because of the responsibility attached to directing it. The institutions and individuals who allocate capital shape how opportunity moves through the world. Their decisions influence which ideas receive support, which communities gain resources, and which structures endure across generations.

Such responsibility cannot rest on technique alone. Skill can navigate markets, but character must guide power.

For this reason, stewardship requires standards strong enough to hold both competence and conscience together. Without such standards, capital becomes merely a force to be optimized. With them, it becomes a force capable of strengthening the systems upon which societies depend.

This realization leads to the final stage of the journey.

If capital carries this weight, and if stewardship requires this depth of character, then a final question becomes unavoidable.

What kind of standard is strong enough to guide those entrusted with directing capital?

That is the question to which the final chapters now turn.

Chapter 13

The Architecture of Capital

Capital does not move only through decisions. It moves through structures.

Every investment, loan, acquisition, or portfolio allocation appears, at first glance, to be the product of individual judgment. Portfolio managers evaluate opportunities. Analysts examine financial statements and industry trends. Investment committees debate risks and potential returns. Executives define strategic priorities, and boards oversee the direction of institutions entrusted with large pools of capital.

Yet none of these decisions occur in isolation. They take place within a framework of rules, incentives, institutions, and technologies that shape how participants interpret opportunity, measure success, and respond to uncertainty. These structures influence not only what decisions are made, but which decisions appear rational, responsible, or even possible in the first place.

Financial systems, therefore, do not operate solely through individual choices. They operate through architecture.

Rules, reporting systems, governance structures, regulatory boundaries, compensation frameworks, and market infrastructure together form the environment through which capital moves. This architecture does not dictate every action taken by financial participants, but it establishes the conditions within which those actions are interpreted, rewarded, and repeated. Over time, these structural conditions shape patterns of behavior that extend far beyond any single institution.

Understanding this architecture is essential to understanding why capital flows through the economy as it does.

Participants inside financial institutions often experience their decisions as expressions of independent judgment. Portfolio managers evaluate investments based on research and analysis. Analysts build models to assess future growth. Executives allocate resources across business lines or asset classes in line with strategic priorities. Each of these activities appears to be guided by professional expertise.

But each decision is shaped by the system in which it operates.

Compensation systems reward certain outcomes. Reporting frameworks determine how performance is measured. Regulatory standards establish boundaries for acceptable activity. Competitive pressures encourage institutions to monitor peer behavior and adapt accordingly. Technology influences both the speed at which decisions must be made and the information available when they are made. These forces rarely command attention in the moment, yet they quietly guide behavior across the system.

The architecture of finance operates much like the structure of a building. The occupants of that building may move freely within its rooms. They can rearrange furniture, open doors, and change the activities taking place inside. Yet the structure determines where the walls stand, how light enters the space, how people circulate, and which areas remain accessible.

In the same way, financial participants make choices within a system whose architecture defines the boundaries of those choices.

Markets, in this sense, are not purely spontaneous environments. They are designed environments. Rules governing trading practices, disclosure obligations, capital standards, compensation frameworks, reporting requirements, and market access collectively shape how participants interact with one another. These arrangements influence which strategies become widely adopted, which risks appear acceptable, and which forms of behavior gradually disappear from the system.

Architecture shapes behavior.

This principle extends far beyond finance. In cities, street and public space design influences how people move and interact. In organizations, governance structures shape decision-making authority and accountability. In financial systems, institutional frameworks shape the movement of capital. Participants may believe they are acting independently, yet their behavior often reflects the structure surrounding them.

One of the clearest examples of this influence appears in the structure of performance measurements within the investment industry. Most asset managers operate under relatively short reporting horizons. Quarterly returns, annual performance rankings, benchmark comparisons, and peer-group analysis influence how firms attract and retain client capital. Institutions that outperform benchmarks often attract additional assets, while those experiencing temporary underperformance may face significant outflows.

These reporting frameworks shape institutional behavior.

Managers must demonstrate competitive results to maintain credibility with clients and within their organizations. Even firms that emphasize long-term investment philosophies still operate within evaluation cycles that highlight short-term outcomes. As a result, strategies often evolve to reflect the cadence of institutional evaluation.

This dynamic does not necessarily arise from poor judgment on the part of individual managers. Many investment professionals recognize that certain opportunities require patience to realize their full potential. Infrastructure development, scientific research, industrial transformation, and emerging technologies often unfold over long horizons. Yet, if capital providers withdraw assets during periods of temporary underperformance, institutions may feel compelled to adjust their strategies to remain aligned with client expectations.

Structural conditions gradually shape behavior, as well.

Over time, these forces influence the kinds of opportunities that attract capital. Investments capable of producing visible results within shorter periods often gain attention more quickly than projects whose benefits emerge over many years. Long-term investment does not disappear, but the architecture of financial evaluation affects how frequently it occurs and how capital is distributed across competing possibilities.

When large numbers of institutions operate within similar evaluation frameworks, capital flows can become synchronized. Asset classes experiencing strong recent performance often attract increasing allocations. Sectors facing temporary weakness may experience capital withdrawals even when their long-term prospects remain fundamentally sound, capital moves toward visible success and away from perceived uncertainty, reinforcing trends already underway.

These synchronized movements contribute to cycles of expansion and contraction.

Regulation represents another powerful component of financial architecture. Governments and regulatory bodies establish frameworks designed to protect investors, maintain market stability, and ensure transparency within financial institutions. These frameworks shape everything from capital requirements for banks to disclosure obligations for publicly traded companies.

These rules strengthen market integrity.

Transparency, accountability, and resilience depend on regulatory frameworks that maintain trust among market participants. But regulation also shapes how institutions organize themselves. Financial institutions do not passively accept regulatory frameworks. They adapt to them. When new rules are introduced, firms adjust business models, capital structures, or investment strategies to remain competitive within the boundaries those rules establish.

This interaction between regulation and institutional adaptation can reshape market structure in unexpected ways.

In the aftermath of the 2008 global financial crisis, for example, regulatory reforms significantly increased banks' capital requirements. As a result, certain financial activities gradually migrated away from traditional banking institutions toward asset managers and other nonbank entities. Over time, this migration contributed to the expansion of what is commonly described as the shadow banking system, a network of financial activity occurring outside traditional banking structures.

This evolution reveals an important feature of financial architecture. It continuously adapts.

Technology adds another layer to this architecture. Advances in computing power, data analytics, and electronic trading platforms have transformed the operation of financial markets. Information now travels across global markets almost instantaneously. Trading strategies can be executed at speeds far beyond human reaction time. Algorithmic systems now participate in a substantial portion of modern market activity.

In many circumstances, these systems provide genuine benefits. They facilitate price discovery, improve execution, and tighten spreads. However, technological innovation also introduces new dynamics. Because algorithms operate according to programmed rules, large numbers of automated systems may respond simultaneously to similar signals. Under certain conditions, this synchronization can amplify market movement.

Events such as the 2010 flash crash revealed how interactions among automated trading systems can produce sudden price dislocations. On May 6, 2010, U.S. equity markets experienced a rapid and severe disruption in which major indices declined sharply within minutes, only to recover much of those losses shortly thereafter. During this brief period, liquidity evaporated across market segments, and individual securities traded at prices that bore little relation to their underlying value.

Subsequent analysis suggested that the event was not caused by a single failure, but by the interaction of multiple high-frequency trading systems responding to rapidly changing conditions. As selling pressure increased, automated systems simultaneously adjusted positions, amplifying price movements rather than absorbing them. Market participants who would normally provide liquidity stepped back, further accelerating the imbalance between buyers and sellers.

Safeguards have since been introduced to reduce such risks, including trading pauses and circuit breakers designed to slow activity during periods of extreme volatility. Yet the episode illustrates a broader point. Technological infrastructure does not merely facilitate markets. It shapes how they behave, particularly under stress. Systems designed for speed and efficiency can, under certain conditions, transmit disruption just as effectively as they transmit information.

Architecture shapes behavior, and stewardship cannot be confined to individual judgment alone. It must extend to the design of the systems through which capital moves.

Stewardship must extend to the design of systems that encourage responsible judgment. Institutions must examine how governance frameworks, reporting standards, regulatory environments, and incentive systems influence the conduct of those responsible for allocating capital. When these structural elements align with long-term stability, financial systems become more resilient.

History demonstrates the importance of maintaining this balance. When compensation systems reward excessive risk-taking, institutions may pursue strategies that generate short-term gains while exposing the system to longer-term vulnerabilities. When transparency is limited, market participants may underestimate risks accumulating within complex structures. When governance is weak, capital can move efficiently while still drifting toward fragility.

Recognizing these dynamics is not optional. It is a prerequisite for designing financial systems that can sustain stability over time.

Institutions that design governance systems emphasizing accountability, transparency, and long-term alignment create environments in which stewardship can flourish. Risk will never disappear from financial markets, but the architecture of finance determines whether risk is carried responsibly or amplified unnecessarily.

Ultimately, financial systems reflect the collective decisions of the societies that construct them. They do not exist as natural phenomena operating independently of human influence. Markets are built, designed, regulated, and sustained by institutions that direct resources across time, industries, and communities.

Because of this, the structure surrounding those decisions matters. The architecture of financial systems does more than facilitate the movement of capital. It shapes the conditions under which capital moves, influencing not only efficiency, but also the stability, trustworthiness, and resilience of the environment those systems create.

Which raises a deeper question.

If the architecture of finance shapes behavior across entire markets, then the principles guiding that architecture matter profoundly. What standards should govern the design of financial systems? What disciplines should shape the incentives and structures through which capital flows? And how might financial systems evolve if stewardship were embedded not only in the character of individuals, but in the architecture of capital itself?

Those questions lead to the next stage.

The Stewardship Standard.

Chapter 14

The Stewardship Standard

Financial systems do not evolve by accident. They evolve through design, adaptation, and the cumulative decisions of the institutions and individuals who participate in them.

Throughout history, the architecture of finance has reflected the conditions of its time. Banking networks that emerged in Renaissance Europe supported the expansion of trade across continents. Capital markets that developed during the Industrial Revolution financed railroads, factories, and the infrastructure required to sustain industrial growth. In the twentieth century, the expansion of global markets and technological innovation allowed capital to move across borders with unprecedented speed and scale.

Each stage of development reshaped the financial system. The next stage will do the same.

The architecture of finance today is the product of decades, and in many respects centuries, of institutional development, regulatory adaptation, technological innovation, and economic transformation. Financial systems are not static. They evolve continuously in response to changing conditions, emerging risks, and new opportunities for capital deployment.

The question facing modern financial institutions is not whether the system will change, but how. It is how it will change, and according to what principles.

Answering that question requires recognizing the forces already reshaping global finance and the responsibilities carried by those entrusted with directing capital within it. Technological innovation, demographic change, globalization, and the expanding scale of institutional capital are redefining the environment in which investment decisions occur. These developments are not isolated trends. Together, they are reshaping the conditions under which capital is allocated and the responsibilities carried by those who guide it.

In such an environment, stewardship becomes more than a philosophical aspiration. It becomes a governing standard.

The Stewardship Standard begins with a simple but decisive recognition. Capital is not merely a financial instrument. It is a force that shapes the structure of economies, the direction of innovation, and the range of opportunities available within societies. Every allocation helps shape the system that future generations will inherit.

For that reason, stewardship requires more than technical competence. It requires principles strong enough to guide capital through periods of transformation.

One of the most powerful drivers of this transformation is technological change. Advances in data analysis, artificial intelligence, and digital infrastructure are reshaping how institutions evaluate investments, manage portfolios, and assess risk. These tools expand analytical capability and accelerate decision-making, allowing institutions to operate with greater precision across increasingly complex systems.

Yet greater capability does not eliminate uncertainty. It changes its form. Models rely on assumptions. Historical data cannot fully anticipate structural change. When institutions rely on similar frameworks, their decisions can become synchronized, amplifying systemic risk. Technology, therefore, increases the importance of judgment rather than replacing it.

This produces a financial environment in which information moves faster, and analysis operates at greater depth. Technology expands insight while increasing the importance of discipline in its application.

The Stewardship Standard requires institutions to recognize that technological sophistication does not eliminate uncertainty. It heightens the importance of disciplined judgment in its management.

Another transformation involves the infrastructure through which financial transactions occur. Digital platforms have expanded access to investment opportunities once largely limited to institutional participants. Individuals can now trade globally from personal devices, participate in crowdfunding initiatives, and allocate capital through digital asset platforms operating outside traditional banking structures.

Greater access can increase liquidity and create opportunities. Entrepreneurs can reach investors across continents. Individuals in emerging economies can participate more directly in global markets.

Yet expanded participation introduces new complexity. Markets must absorb participants with varying levels of experience, different time horizons, and unequal informational advantages. Regulatory frameworks must evolve to ensure that broader access does not introduce new vulnerabilities or expose participants to risks they cannot reasonably evaluate.

The democratization of finance, therefore, carries both opportunity and obligation. Stewardship requires that expanded access be matched with structures that preserve market integrity.

A related development involves decentralized financial infrastructure. Blockchain systems and distributed ledger technologies enable transactions without the need for traditional intermediaries. Settlement processes that once required multiple layers of verification can be streamlined, and ownership records can be maintained across distributed systems.

These innovations may alter the role of established institutions, but they do not eliminate the need for oversight, experience, or disciplined risk management. Technology may change how capital moves. It does not remove the need for responsible stewardship.

Demographic change represents another force reshaping financial systems. In many developed economies, populations are aging. This increases the importance of retirement systems, long-term savings vehicles, and institutions capable of managing capital across extended time horizons. Pension funds, insurance companies, and sovereign wealth funds oversee enormous pools of capital intended to support individuals and societies for decades to come.

The scale of these responsibilities is significant. Their allocation decisions shape the long-term structure of capital markets.

At the same time, younger generations are bringing new expectations regarding how capital should be allocated. Many investors now consider not only financial performance but also the broader consequences of investment decisions. As capital shifts toward new priorities, those allocations influence the direction of economic development.

Globalization continues to shape financial evolution. Capital moves across borders with extraordinary speed, creating opportunities in emerging economies alongside established markets in developed regions. At the same time, institutions must navigate geopolitical risk, regulatory differences, and currency dynamics when allocating capital internationally.

These cross-border flows create both opportunity and complexity. Access to global capital can accelerate development. Yet rapid shifts in allocation can also introduce instability. Managing these dynamics requires institutions capable of operating with discipline across multiple systems simultaneously.

Another defining feature of the modern financial system is the increasing scale of capital itself. Institutional investors now oversee portfolios measured in trillions of dollars. As these pools grow larger, their influence on global markets expands with them.

At sufficient scale, capital allocation is no longer merely a technical exercise. It becomes a form of economic influence. Decisions made by large allocators shape industries, infrastructure development, technological progress, and the distribution of opportunity across regions.

In such an environment, disciplined capital deployment becomes essential. The Stewardship Standard requires institutions to combine rigorous financial analysis with an awareness of systemic consequence. Capital must be directed in ways that sustain financial stability while supporting productive economic activity.

This standard does not eliminate competition or innovation. Markets remain environments of experimentation, risk-taking, and strategic advantage. But stewardship introduces an additional discipline. It asks whether capital is being directed in ways that strengthen the systems upon which long-term prosperity depends.

That is the heart of the standard.

It is not a rejection of performance. It is not a substitute for rigor. It is the recognition that capital cannot be directed responsibly without a governing framework equal to its consequences.

Throughout this book, we have examined the movement of capital, the expansion of financial systems, the power of allocation, the influence of incentives, institutional drift, early warning signals, the role of psychology, the illusion of control, the fragility created by complexity, the concentration of capital power, and the character required of those entrusted with directing it.

For this reason, the stewardship of capital carries profound responsibility.

Those who direct capital are not merely managing financial resources. They are shaping the economic future.

Capital carries weight not only because of its financial value, but because of the consequences attached to directing it. To recognize that weight is to understand that every allocation contributes to the structure of the world that follows.

The future of finance will not be written through innovation alone, regulation alone, or competition alone. It will be shaped by the judgment exercised by those who guide capital through the systems we have built.

The durability of those systems will depend on whether those entrusted with capital choose to carry its weight with discipline, responsibility, and stewardship.

That is the standard.

And that is the weight that must be carried.

Chapter 15

Carrying the Weight of Capital

Capital is often discussed as though it were abstract. In financial discourse, it appears as numbers moving across screens, prices rising and falling, portfolios shifting, and balance sheets expanding and contracting. Analysts revise forecasts, institutions publish results, and markets respond to new information with remarkable speed. Within this continuous stream of data, capital can appear detached from the realities it ultimately shapes.

Yet capital is never truly abstract. Behind every dollar lies a human story: savings accumulated over years of work. Pension funds safeguard workers' retirement savings. Endowments preserve donors' intentions. Sovereign wealth funds manage national assets on behalf of citizens whose collective productivity generated those reserves. In every case, the capital allocated represents the accumulated effort of individuals and communities whose futures are tied to the decisions of financial institutions.

To allocate capital responsibly is therefore to acknowledge the trust embedded within it. Those who provide capital do so with the expectation that it will be managed prudently and directed toward productive purposes. They rely on financial professionals not only for technical expertise, but for judgment that protects the long-term interests of those whose resources are at stake.

This responsibility extends across generations. Decisions made today influence economic conditions that may persist for decades. Infrastructure financed today may serve communities for half a century. Investments in technological innovation may shape industries that define the next era of development. Capital allocation links present decisions with future realities in ways few professions encounter so directly.

As financial systems grow more interconnected and capital flows increase in scale, the consequences of allocation become more significant. Institutions responsible for guiding these flows must operate with an awareness that extends beyond immediate financial outcomes. They must consider not only the performance of individual investments, but the stability of the systems within which markets operate.

Healthy financial systems depend on trust between participants. Investors must believe that institutions operate with integrity and that markets function according to rules applied consistently across participants. Regulators must maintain frameworks that promote transparency while enabling innovation. Participants must trust that the structures connecting them remain reliable even during periods of stress.

When these conditions hold, financial systems can channel capital productively into the activities that sustain economic growth. When trust erodes, instability often follows. History repeatedly demonstrates that financial crises begin with a breakdown of confidence within the system itself. When participants question the reliability of institutions or the transparency of markets, liquidity can withdraw rapidly, and the fragility that once remained hidden becomes visible.

Stewardship, therefore, contributes directly to systemic stability. Those responsible for allocating capital influence not only the performance of their own institutions, but the confidence that sustains financial markets more broadly.

By maintaining transparency, exercising disciplined risk management, and recognizing the broader consequences of their decisions, stewards strengthen the foundations upon which markets depend.

Most financial decisions occur quietly within investment committees, research teams, and risk discussions. Analysts evaluate emerging industries. Portfolio managers debate allocation strategies. Institutions assess tradeoffs between short-term performance and long-term resilience. Individually, these decisions appear routine. Collectively, they shape the economic environment in which societies operate.

When capital is allocated thoughtfully, it becomes a catalyst for progress. When it is directed carelessly, it contributes to instability or wasted potential. The difference lies not in the existence of capital, but in the character of those who guide it.

Financial history repeatedly illustrates how institutional character influences outcomes. Organizations that emphasize transparency, prudence, and long-term thinking tend to strengthen stability. Institutions driven primarily by short-term advantage may contribute to cycles of excess that ultimately undermine the markets on which they depend.

Leadership within financial institutions, therefore, carries significance that extends beyond performance metrics. Leaders shape the culture through which decisions are made. They establish expectations regarding risk, transparency, and accountability, and they determine whether institutions encourage thoughtful analysis or reward behavior that prioritizes immediate results over sustainable growth.

For those entering the field of finance, this perspective offers an important reminder. Technical expertise remains essential. Understanding financial markets requires analytical skill, quantitative tools, and knowledge of economic systems. Yet these capabilities alone do not define responsible financial leadership. Equally important are qualities that cannot be reduced to formulas: judgment, integrity, patience, and the willingness to question prevailing assumptions when markets appear most confident.

Ultimately, the future of finance will not be determined by technological innovation alone, regulatory reform alone, or competition alone. It will be shaped by the principles embraced by those entrusted with directing capital.

If stewardship becomes central to financial decision-making, if institutions recognize the responsibility inherent in the resources they manage, capital can serve as a force for durable economic progress. It can support innovation that improves human life, infrastructure that strengthens communities, and enterprises that expand opportunities across societies.

But this outcome is not automatic. It depends on the choices individuals and institutions make every day in financial markets. To carry the weight of capital is not simply to manage money. It is to recognize the responsibility embedded within the resources entrusted to financial institutions and to act with the discipline required to direct that responsibility wisely.

Because capital will always shape the future. And the character of those who guide it will determine what kind of future it becomes.

The Stewardship of Capital

Capital carries weight. It carries the accumulated effort of millions of people who work, save, build, and contribute to the economic systems that sustain modern societies. Every dollar entrusted to financial institutions represents time, discipline, and the expectation that those resources will be directed with care. To guide capital is therefore to guide the expression of human effort itself.

Financial markets often obscure this reality. Within trading screens and performance reports, capital appears as numbers moving across balance sheets. Yet behind those numbers lie the ambitions of entrepreneurs, the security of workers, the stability of institutions, and the future opportunities of generations yet to come. Those who allocate capital, therefore, do more than manage financial resources. Their decisions determine which businesses expand, which technologies mature, and which possibilities are given the time and support required to become real. In this way, capital shapes the structure of economies and the direction of progress.

This influence carries responsibility. Capital is not possessed in isolation. It is entrusted. Pension systems safeguard workers' savings. Endowments preserve philanthropic commitments. Sovereign funds manage national resources. In each case, capital reflects effort already given and expectation not yet realized. To allocate capital responsibly is to recognize that trust.

The modern financial system rarely speaks in these terms. It emphasizes performance, efficiency, and scale. These disciplines are necessary, but they are not sufficient. Financial systems do not endure on technical capability alone. They depend on judgment, discipline, and a sustained awareness of consequence. This is the role of stewardship.

Stewardship asks those who guide capital to look beyond immediate returns and consider the structures their decisions help create. It requires clarity when conditions encourage excess, discipline when incentives reward speed, and responsibility when the consequences of allocation extend beyond the moment in which decisions are made.

Markets function most effectively when trust is preserved. When participants believe that capital is directed with discipline, systems remain stable, innovation is supported, and opportunity expands. When that trust weakens, fragility often follows. For this reason, stewardship strengthens not only individual institutions but the financial system itself.

The future of finance will not be determined by innovation alone, nor by regulation alone. It will be shaped by the standards applied by those entrusted with directing capital. Each allocation represents a choice about what will be built, what will endure, and what will be left behind. Over time, those choices accumulate, shaping the economic environment that future generations will inherit.

To steward capital is to participate in that construction. It is to recognize that financial decisions are not confined to balance sheets but extend into the structure of the world that follows. Capital will continue to move. Markets will continue to evolve. Systems will continue to grow in scale and complexity.

The question is not whether capital carries weight.

The question is whether those who direct it are prepared to carry it.

Author's Reflections

"The ultimate test of a system is not how it performs, but how it endures over time."

I didn't set out to write a book.

I set out to understand something that didn't sit right.

Years inside financial systems brought me close enough to see how decisions are made, how capital moves, and how outcomes are defined. On the surface, everything is structured around performance, efficiency, and return. But underneath that, something else is happening.

Capital doesn't stay where it's placed.

It shapes what gets built.
It shapes what survives.
It shapes what becomes normal.

This changed how I saw everything.

Capital is not neutral, and the responsibility for what it builds cannot be separated from those who direct it.

Shepherds of Capital was built from that place, not as an idea, but as a response.

Acknowledgements

No work of this nature is completed in isolation.

My deepest gratitude begins with my sister, Jill Panetta. Your encouragement remained constant throughout this process. You challenged me to move forward with conviction, to trust both my judgment and my faith, and to complete what I had begun even when the path forward was not fully visible.

I am equally grateful to my parents, Maureen and Kenneth. From you, I learned discipline, commitment, and integrity, which have shaped the perspective from which this work was written.

Through you, my nephews, Nicholas, Charlie, and William, and my brother-in-law, Randolph, I am reminded of the importance of building with future generations in mind. The ideas explored in this book are grounded in that responsibility.

A close circle of friends surrounds me, offering consistent support and belief throughout this process. Stephanie, Ernest, Jenny, Jane, Carol-Lynne, Kathy, Kim, and Simon, thank you for standing alongside me as this work took shape.

To the board members of the Shepherds of Capital Foundation, your discipline, perspective, and commitment continue to shape the standard this work reflects.

I am grateful to Joey, whose design work shaped the cover and website of this book, and to Elizabeth, whose care in the interior layout gave every page its clarity and structure.

And to the many colleagues who have contributed to my thinking over time. Some demonstrated the standards toward which the system should aspire. Many did not.

This work exists because that gap remains.

www.ingramcontent.com/pod-product-compliance
Ingram Content Group UK Ltd.
Pitfield, Milton Keynes, MK11 3LW, UK
UKHW020030121026
15625UKWH00042B/233

9 798995 772347